Cookies Candies
&
Confections

Butter-Mint Kiss Cookies
Orange-Pecan Kiss Cookies
Chocolate Kiss Cookies

Peanut Butter Kiss Bars
Coconut-Cherry Kiss Cookies
Oatmeal Kiss Cookies

Cookies, Candies
&
Confections

Favorite Recipes Press
a division of
Great American Opportunities, Inc.

Recipes for cover on pages 65, 66, 83, 84 and 89.

◀ *Recipes on pages 13,15 and 17.*

Credits

Editorial Staff

Editorial Manager:	Mary Jane Blount
Cookbook Editors:	Georgia Brazil
	Mary Cummings
	Jane Hinshaw
	LaNita Stout
Typography:	William Maul
	Edna Prowell

Photography

Hershey Foods Corp.; The Kellogg Company; The Quaker Oats Company; Diamond Walnut Growers; Planters Cocktail Peanuts; Skippy peanut butter; United Dairy Industry Association; Ocean Spray Cranberries, Inc.; California Apricot Advisory Board; United Fresh Fruit and Vegetable Association; Florida Department of Citrus; Karo corn syrup.

Copyright © 1986 by Great American Opportunities, Inc.
P. O. Box 77, Nashville, Tennessee 37202

Library of Congress Catalog Number is as follows: 86-8875
ISBN: 0-87197-209-3

Manufactured in the United States of America
First Printing 1986

Contents

Cookie Know-How

D o you remember your very first cooking venture? You probably began with a recipe from your mother's recipe file, one of your favorite cookies! Easy to prepare and a treat for all ages, there is not better way to learn to cook! By following the recipe carefully, beginners can turn out beautiful cookies that are perfect for gifts or the cookie jar.

Basic Guidelines for Cookie-Making Success

◆ Read your recipe carefully *before* beginning.

◆ Use standard measuring untensils and measure *carefully*. No guessing!

◆ Prepare your cookie sheet. Most all cookies are baked on *greased* cookie sheets. Cookies containing considerable amounts of shortening are baked on ungreased cookie sheets.

◆ For best results have all ingredients at room temperature.

◆ Mix cookie dough exactly as instructed in the recipe.

◆ Bake cookies near the center of the oven to allow plenty of space for the heat to circulate.

◆ Set your timer for the minimum baking time given. *Bar cookies* are done when the sides shrink from the pan or when the top springs back when lightly touched. *Soft cookies* will also spring back when touched. *Crisp cookies* are done when fairly firm and lightly browned around the edges.

◆ Unless otherwide directed, remove cookies from the cookie sheet immediately after baking. Using a wide spatula, place cookies in a single layer on wire racks to cool.

◆ Never store soft cookies and crisp cookies together. Soft cookies should be stored in an airtight container. If *soft cookies* become dry, add moisture by placing an apple or orange slice in the container for a day or so. Store *crisp cookies* in a container with a loose fitting cover. If they become limp, freshen in a 300-degree oven for about 5 minutes before serving. *Bar cookies* may be stored in the baking pan covered with foil.

Cookies-on-the Go

Soft cookies are better travelers than crisp cookies. To avoid damage during shipping, follow these tips.

◆ Use a strong cardboard box or metal container lined with waxed paper or foil.

◆ Place a layer of crumpled waxed paper in box. Pack wrapped pairs of cookies in rows, filling in spaces with more crumpled waxed paper. Place a layer of crumpled waxed paper between layers of cookies, adding an extra layer of waxed paper on top.

Bar Cookie Magic

Pan Size	Number of cuts		Yield
	Lengthwise	Crosswise	
8x8-inch	3	3	1⅓ dozen
	3	5	2 dozen
9x13-inch	2	7	2 dozen
	5	5	3 dozen
	7	5	4 dozen
10x15-inch	3	8	3 dozen
	3	11	4 dozen
	3	14	5 dozen
	7	8	6 dozen

ALMOND BUTTERCUPS

2 c. flour
¼ tsp. salt
¾ c. sugar
½ c. butter, softened
2 eggs
1 tsp. vanilla extract
½ tsp. almond extract
½ c. almond paste

Mix flour, salt and ½ cup sugar in bowl. Add butter and 1 egg; mix well. Press over bottom and sides of miniature muffin cups. Beat 1 egg in small mixer bowl until frothy. Add ¼ cup sugar and flavorings gradually; beat until thickened. Blend in almond paste. Spoon 1 teaspoonful into each prepared miniature muffin cup. Bake at 350 degrees for 20 minutes or until golden brown. Cool in pan for 5 minutes. Remove to wire rack to cool completely.
Yield: 3 dozen.

Fran Kowalik, New York

ALMOND CRESCENT COOKIES

1 lb. butter, softened
1⅓ c. sugar
8 oz. almonds, ground
3½ c. flour
Confectioner's sugar

Cream butter and sugar in large bowl until light and fluffy. Add almonds and flour; mix well. Chill until firm. Shape into crescents on ungreased cookie sheet. Bake at 375 degrees until golden brown. Cool on wire rack. Coat with confectioners' sugar.
Yield: 10 dozen.

Beate Sachnowitz, Texas

JAPANESE ALMOND COOKIES

2¾ c. sifted flour
1 c. sugar
½ tsp. soda
½ tsp. salt
1 c. butter
1 egg, slightly beaten
1 tsp. almond extract
⅓ c. slivered almonds

Sift flour, sugar, soda and salt into bowl. Cut in butter until crumbly. Add remaining ingredients; mix well. Shape into small balls. Place on ungreased cookie sheet. Press to flatten slightly. Bake at 325 degrees for 15 minutes. Cool on wire rack.
Yield: 5 dozen.

Dottie Wilson, South Carolina

ALMOND SPRITZ

1 c. butter, softened
¾ c. sugar
1 egg
2½ c. flour, sifted
½ tsp. baking powder
Dash of salt
1 tsp. almond extract

Cream butter and sugar in bowl until light and fluffy. Add egg; beat well. Add sifted dry ingredients gradually. Stir in almond flavoring. Fill cookie press fitted with desired tip. Press 1½ inches apart on lightly greased cookie sheet. Bake at 350 degrees for 10 minutes or until light brown. Cool on wire rack.
Yield: 5 dozen.

Sherry Sanders, Alabama

ANISE COOKIES

2 c. sugar
2 c. shortening
2 c. molasses
4 tsp. ginger
2 eggs
4 tsp. soda
1 tsp. salt
1 tsp. anise oil
10 c. (about) flour

Combine first 5 ingredients in large bowl; mix well. Add soda dissolved in 1 cup boiling water; mix well. Beat in salt and anise oil. Stir in enough flour to make stiff dough. Roll on floured surface; cut as desired. Place on greased cookie sheet. Bake at 350 degrees for 8 minutes. Cool on wire rack.
Yield: 6 dozen.

Joan Murphy, Montana

FRESH APPLE BARS

1¾ c. sugar
1 c. oil
3 eggs
1 tsp. vanilla extract
2 c. flour
1 tsp. each salt, soda, cinnamon
2 c. sliced apples
1 c. chopped nuts
Confectioners' sugar

Blend first 4 ingredients in large bowl. Sift in flour, salt, soda, and cinnamon; mix well. Fold in apples and nuts. Pour into greased 9x13-inch baking pan. Bake at 375 degrees for 45 minutes. Cool. Sprinkle with confectioners' sugar. Cut into 2-inch bars.

Susan Levi, Ohio

APPLESAUCE-RAISIN BARS

¼ c. shortening
⅔ c. packed brown sugar
1 c. applesauce
1 egg
1 c. flour
1 tsp. soda
½ tsp. salt
1 tsp. pumpkin pie spice
½ c. raisins
3 tbsp. butter
1½ c. confectioners' sugar
1 tsp. vanilla extract
1 tbsp. milk

Combine first 4 ingredients in bowl; mix well. Add mixture of flour, soda, salt and spice; mix well. Stir in raisins. Spread in greased 9x13-inch baking pan. Bake at 350 degrees for 25 minutes. Cool in pan. Cook butter in saucepan over medium heat until light brown; remove from heat. Add confectioners' sugar, vanilla and milk; mix well. Spread over cooled baked layer. Cut into bars.

Theresa Fox, Ohio

APRICOT BARS

½ c. margarine
1½ c. graham cracker crumbs
1 6-oz. package dried apricots, chopped
1 can sweetened condensed milk
1 3½-oz. can flaked coconut
½ c. coarsely chopped nuts

Melt margarine in 9x13-inch baking dish. Layer crumbs and apricots in prepared dish. Pour condensed milk evenly over layers. Top with coconut and nuts; press gently. Bake at 350 degrees for 25 minutes or until lightly browned. Cool. Cut into squares.

Norita Adam, Oklahoma

APRICOT BLONDIES

½ c. butter, softened
2 c. packed brown sugar
2 eggs
1½ tsp. vanilla extract
1¼ c. sifted flour
½ c. oats
½ c. chopped dried apricots
¼ c. chopped nuts

Cream butter and brown sugar in bowl until light and fluffy. Add eggs and vanilla; mix well. Mix in flour, oats, apricots and nuts; mix well. Spread in two 8-inch square pans. Bake at 350 degrees for 25 minutes or until firm. Cool. Cut into squares.

Photograph for this recipe on page 13.

APRICOT THIMBLES

1½ c. margarine, softened
1 8-oz. package cream cheese, softened
1½ c. sugar
2 eggs
2 tbsp. lemon juice
2 tsp. grated lemon rind
4½ c. flour
1½ tsp. baking powder
Apricot preserves
Confectioners' sugar

Combine first 3 ingredients in mixer bowl; mix well. Blend in eggs, lemon juice and rind. Add flour and baking powder; mix well. Chill in refrigerator. Shape tablespoonfuls into balls. Place on ungreased cookie sheet. Flatten slightly, indenting center. Fill center with 1 teaspoon preserves. Bake at 350 degrees for 15 minutes. Cool on wire rack. Sprinkle with confectioners' sugar. Yield: 7 dozen.

Carol Jacobsen, Illinois

BANANA BARS

1½ c. sugar
¾ c. packed brown sugar
2 c. sifted flour
½ c. butter
2 sm. bananas, thinly sliced
¾ c. coconut
1 tsp. each salt, soda, cinnamon
¼ tsp. nutmeg
½ c. sour cream
1 egg

Combine sugar, brown sugar and flour in bowl. Cut in butter until crumbly. Reserve ½ cup mixture. Press remaining mixture into lightly greased 9x13-inch baking pan. Combine remaining ingredients in mixer bowl; mix well. Beat at medium speed for 1 minute. Pour over crumb layer. Top with reserved crumb mixture. Bake at 350 degrees for 30 minutes or until brown. Cool. Cut into bars.

Dawn Haug, Indiana

◆◆◆◆◆◆◆◆◆◆◆◆◆◆◆◆◆◆◆◆◆◆◆◆◆◆◆◆◆◆◆◆◆◆

Hint: *Use recommended pan size for bar cookies. Too large or too small pans may alter baking time or quality of cookies.*

◆◆◆◆◆◆◆◆◆◆◆◆◆◆◆◆◆◆◆◆◆◆◆◆◆◆◆◆◆◆◆◆◆◆

BERLINERKRANZE

1 c. melted butter
½ c. sugar
2 egg yolks
2 hard-boiled egg yolks, mashed
2 c. flour
1 tsp. vanilla extract
1 egg white, slightly beaten
Crushed loaf sugar

Combine first 6 ingredients in bowl; mix well. Chill for 1 hour. Shape into pencil-sized pieces. Bend each into single knot. Dip into egg white then into sugar. Place on large ungreased baking sheet. Bake at 400 degrees for 10 minutes or until golden brown. Cool on wire rack. Yield: 6 dozen.

LaVerne Paidar, Iowa

BISCOCHITOS

2 c. lard
1½ c. sugar
2 eggs
2 tsp. aniseed
6 c. flour
1 tbsp. baking powder
1 tsp. salt
½ c. Peach Brandy
1 tsp. cinnamon

Cream lard and 1 cup sugar in bowl until light and fluffy. Add eggs and aniseed; mix well. Add mixture of flour, baking powder and salt alternately with Brandy, mixing well after each addition. Roll ½ inch thick on floured surface. Cut as desired. Sprinkle with mixture of cinnamon and remaining ½ cup sugar. Place on ungreased cookie sheet. Bake at 350 degrees for 10 minutes. Cool on wire rack. Coat with additional cinnamon-sugar before serving.

Aileen Garcia, New Mexico

BLUEBERRY BARS

½ c. shortening
½ c. margarine, softened
1½ c. sugar
4 eggs
1 tsp. vanilla extract
3 c. flour
1½ tsp. baking powder
½ tsp. salt
2 tbsp. milk
3 c. blueberries
1 recipe confectioners' sugar glaze

Cream shortening, margarine and sugar in bowl until light and fluffy. Stir in eggs and vanilla. Add combined dry ingredients and milk; mix well. Spread half the batter in greased 15x17-inch baking pan. Spoon blueberries over batter. Spread remaining batter over top. Bake at 350 degrees for 30 minutes. Spread glaze over warm baked layer. Cool. Cut into bars.

Anita M. Forte, Minnesota

BROWN SUGAR COOKIES

1 c. packed brown sugar
½ c. shortening
¼ c. buttermilk
1 egg
1¾ c.flour
½ tsp. 1 each soda, salt
¼ c. butter
2 c. confectioners' sugar
1 tsp. vanilla extract
1 to 2 tbsp. milk

Cream shortening; brown sugar, buttermilk and egg in bowl. Stir in mixture of flour, soda and salt. Chill for 1 hour or longer. Drop by teaspoonfuls onto greased cookie sheet. Bake at 400 degrees for 8 minutes or until firm. Cool on wire rack. Brown butter in skillet. Mix with confectioners' sugar, vanilla and enough milk to make of spreading consistency. Frost cooled cookies. Yield: 3 dozen.

Variations:

Applesauce Drops — Substitute ½ cup applesauce for buttermilk and add 1 cup raisins, 1 teaspoon cinnamon and ¼ teaspoon cloves.
Chocolate Chip-Cherry Drops — Add ½ cup chocolate chips, ½ cup chopped maraschino cherries, ½ cup coconut and 1 or ½ cup chopped nuts.
Wheat Cereal Drops — Substitute 1 cup oats and ½ cup whole wheat flakes for 1 cup flour and add ½ cup chopped salted peanuts.
Whole Wheat Drops — Substitute whole wheat flour. Do not refrigerate dough.
Date-Nut Cookies — Add ¼ teaspoon cinnamon to dough. Make indentation in center of each drop. Till with cooked mixture of 2 cups chopped dates, ¾ cup sugar, ½ cup chopped nuts and ¾ cup water.

Elva Barnard, Nebraska

BURNT SUGAR BARS

1¾ c. sugar
½ c. melted butter
2 eggs
1 tsp. vanilla extract

2¼ c. flour
2 tsp. baking powder
¼ tsp. salt
½ c. chopped nuts
1 tbsp. melted butter
1 c. sifted confectioners' sugar
Milk

Cook ½ cup sugar in heavy skillet over low heat until golden brown, stirring constantly. Stir in ½ cup boiling water gradually. Heat until sugar dissolves, stirring constantly. Cook for 5 minutes longer or until reduced to ⅓ cup. Cool. Blend ½ cup butter and 1¼ cups sugar in bowl. Add eggs 1 at a time, mixing well after each addition. Add vanilla and 3 tablespoons sugar syrup; mix well. Add mixture of flour, baking powder and salt. Stir in nuts. Spread in greased 10x15-inch baking pan. Bake at 350 degrees for 13 minutes or until brown. Cool. Blend remaining sugar syrup with 1 tablespoon butter, confectioners' sugar and enough milk to make of spreading consistency. Spread over cooled baked layer. Cut into bars.

Pat Blake, New Mexico

BUTTER MINT COOKIES

1 c. butter, softened
1 c. crushed butter mints
2 c. flour
1 tbsp. sugar

Cream butter in large mixer bowl. Add butter mints and flour; beat at low speed until well blended. Chill in refrigerator. Roll on waxed paper into 9-inch square. Sprinkle with sugar. Cut into 1½-inch squares; place on ungreased cookie sheet. Bake at 300 degrees for 18 minutes or until light brown. Do not overbake. Cool on wire rack. Yield: 3 dozen.

Micaela Callahan, Nebraska

BUTTER-MINT KISS COOKIES

1 c. butter, softened
½ c. sugar
1 tsp. vanilla extract
¼ tsp. mint extract
2 egg yolks
2 c. flour
½ tsp. baking powder
¼ tsp. salt
Red and green food coloring
48 milk chocolate kisses

Cream first 5 ingredients in bowl until light and fluffy. Add mixture of flour, baking powder and salt gradually, blending well after each addition. Divide into 2 portions. Tint 1 portion pink and 1 portion green. Shape into 1-inch balls. Roll in additional sugar. Place on ungreased cookie sheet; flatten to ½-inch thickness. Bake at 350 degrees for 10 minutes. Remove from oven. Place chocolate kiss in center of each cookie; press lightly. Cool on wire rack. Yield: 4 dozen.

Photograph for this recipe on page 1.

BUTTER-NUT KISSES

½ c. butter, softened
½ c. sugar
1 egg
1 tsp. vanilla extract
1¼ c. flour
¼ tsp. soda
⅛ tsp. salt
½ c. finely ground nuts
30 Hershey kisses

Cream butter, sugar, egg and vanilla in bowl until light and fluffy. Add mixture of flour, soda and salt; mix well. Shape into 1-inch balls. Roll in nuts. Place on ungreased cookie sheet. Bake at 350 degrees for 10 minutes or until almost set. Press chocolate kiss into center of each cookie. Cool on wire rack. Chill until chocolate is set. Yield: 2½ dozen.

Photograph for this recipe on page 36.

BUTTERSCOTCH PINWHEELS

1 6-oz. package semisweet chocolate chips
¼ c. shortening
1 can sweetened condensed milk
1 c. flour
1 tsp. vanilla extract
1 6-oz. package butterscotch chips
Confectioners' sugar
½ c. chopped walnuts

Melt chocolate chips and 2 tablespoons shortening in saucepan over low heat, stirring constantly. Remove from heat. Stir in condensed milk, flour and vanilla. Spread in greased 10x15-inch baking pan lined with greased waxed paper. Bake at 325 degrees for 8 minutes. Melt butterscotch chips and 2 tablespoons shortening in saucepan. Turn baked layer onto towel sprinkled with confectioners' sugar. Spread with butterscotch mixture; sprinkle with walnuts. Roll as for jelly roll from long side. Cool. Wrap in plastic wrap. Chill in refrigerator. Cut into ¼-inch slices. Yield: 4½ dozen.

Claire Gumert, Texas

ALMOND BROWNIES

½ c. butter, softened
1 c. sugar
2 eggs
2 sq. unsweetened chocolate, melted
1 tsp. vanilla extract
1½ c. flour
1 c. chopped almonds

Cream butter and sugar in bowl until light and fluffy. Add eggs; mix well. Blend in chocolate, vanilla and flour. Stir in ½ cup almonds. Spread in greased 8-inch square baking pan. Sprinkle with remaining ½ cup almonds. Bake at 350 degrees until nearly set in center. Cool. Cut into squares.

Cheryl Peters, Georgia

APPLESAUCE BROWNIES

½ c. shortening
1½ c. sugar
2 eggs
2 c. applesauce
2 c. flour
2 tbsp. cocoa
1½ tsp. soda
½ tsp. each salt, cinnamon
2 tbsp. sugar
1 6-oz. package chocolate chips
½ c. chopped nuts

Cream shortening and 1½ cups sugar in mixer bowl until light and fluffy. Add eggs; mix well. Add applesauce and mixture of sifted flour, cocoa, soda, salt and cinnamon. Beat for 1 minute. Pour into greased 9x13-inch baking pan. Sprinkle remaining ingredients over top. Bake at 350 degrees for 35 minutes. Cool. Cut into squares.

Dorothy Franks, Ohio

APRICOT BROWNIES

⅔ c. dried apricots
¼ c. sugar
1⅓ c. flour
½ c. butter, softened
2 eggs, well beaten
1 c. packed brown sugar
½ tsp. baking powder
¼ tsp. salt
1 tsp. vanilla extract
½ c. chopped nuts
Confectioners' sugar

Rinse apricots. Place in saucepan with water to cover. Boil for 10 minutes; drain. Cool and chop. Combine sugar with 1 cup flour in bowl. Cut in butter until crumbly. Press into greased 9-inch square baking pan. Bake at 350 degrees for 25 minutes or until light brown. Combine eggs and brown sugar in bowl; beat well. Sift ⅓ cup flour with baking powder and salt. Add flour mixture to egg mixture gradually; mix well. Stir in vanilla, nuts and apricots. Spread over baked layer. Bake at 350 degrees for 30 minutes. Cool. Cut into squares. Sprinkle with confectioners' sugar.

Esther Moorhead, Oklahoma

BUTTERMILK BROWNIES

2 sticks margarine
½ c. cocoa
2 c. flour
2 c. sugar
½ tsp. salt
½ c. buttermilk
2 eggs, beaten
1 tsp. soda
2 tsp. vanilla extract
⅓ c. buttermilk
1 16-oz. package confectioners' sugar
1 c. chopped nuts (opt.)

Combine 1 stick margarine, ¼ cup cocoa and 1 cup water in saucepan. Bring to a boil; mix well. Pour over mixture of flour, sugar and salt in bowl. Add ½ cup buttermilk, eggs, soda and 1 teaspoon vanilla; mix well. Pour into greased and floured 10x15-inch baking pan. Bake at 400 degrees for 20 minutes. Combine remaining 1 stick margarine, ¼ cup cocoa and ⅓ cup buttermilk in saucepan. Bring to a boil; blend well. Remove from heat. Add remaining ingredients; mix until creamy. Spread on hot brownies. Cool. Cut into squares.

Lana J. Crawford, Texas

CHOCOLATE CHIP BLOND BROWNIES

⅓ c. melted butter
1 c. packed brown sugar
1 egg, beaten
1 tsp. vanilla extract
1 c. sifted flour
½ tsp. baking powder
Pinch of soda
½ tsp. salt
½ c. chopped nuts
½ c. chocolate chips

Combine butter and brown sugar in saucepan; mix well. Stir in egg and vanilla. Add next 4 ingredients; mix well. Fold in nuts. Spread in greased 9x9-inch baking pan. Sprinkle with chocolate chips. Bake at 350 degrees for 1 minute. Cut through dough with knife to marbleize. Bake for 19 minutes longer. Cool. Cut into squares.

Ruth Mitchell, Tennessee

◆◆◆◆◆◆◆◆◆◆◆◆◆◆◆◆◆◆◆◆◆◆◆◆◆◆◆◆◆◆◆

Hint: *To store bar cookies, remove from pan in 1 piece. Wrap tightly, and store as desired. Cut into bars before serving.*

◆◆◆◆◆◆◆◆◆◆◆◆◆◆◆◆◆◆◆◆◆◆◆◆◆◆◆◆◆◆◆

BROWNIE MIX PLUS

  1   15-oz. package fudge brownie mix
  ½ c. chopped pecans (opt.)
  ¼ c. chopped maraschino cherries (opt.)
  1 c. chopped dates (opt.)
  3 tbsp. chunky peanut butter (opt.)

Prepare brownie mix according to package directions, adding 1 or more of the optional ingredients. Bake according to package directions. Cool. Cut into bars.

Variations:
Orange Brownies — Substitute ¼ cup orange juice and grated rind of 1 orange for ¼ cup water.
Mint Brownies — Arrange 16 chocolate covered peppermint patties on hot brownies. Bake for 1 minute or until softened. Swirl over top with knife. Cut into squares when cool.

Connie Brown, Tennessee

DOUBLE CHOCOLATE BROWNIES

  ½ c. butter, softened
  ¾ c. sugar
  1 egg
  ½ c. sour cream
  1 tsp. vanilla extract
  1 c. flour
  ¼ c. cocoa
  ¼ tsp. soda
  ¼ tsp. salt
  1 c. Hershey's miniature chocolate chips
  Easy Brownie Frosting

Cream first 3 ingredients in bowl until light and fluffy. Add sour cream and vanilla; beat well. Combine dry ingredients in bowl. Add to creamed mixture; blend well. Stir in chocolate chips. Spread in greased 9-inch square baking dish. Bake at 350 degrees for 30 to 35 minutes or until brownies test almost done. Cool. Frost with Easy Brownie Frosting. Sprinkle with additional chocolate chips and nuts.

Easy Brownie Frosting
  3 tbsp. butter, softened
  3 tbsp. cocoa
  ½ tsp. vanilla extract
  1¼ c. confectioners' sugar
  2 tbsp. milk

Cream butter and cocoa in small mixer bowl until light and fluffy. Add vanilla, confectioners' sugar and milk. Beat until of spreading consistency.

Photograph for this recipe on page 2.

FUDGE-NUT BROWNIES

  ⅔ c. butter, softened
  ½ c. sugar
  1 c. packed brown sugar
  4 eggs
  3 oz. unsweetened chocolate, melted
  2 tsp. vanilla extract
  1 c. sifted flour
  1 tsp. salt
  1½ c. oats
  1 c. chopped nuts

Cream butter and sugars in bowl until light and fluffy. Add eggs, chocolate and vanilla; mix well. Sift in flour and salt; mix well. Stir in oats and nuts. Pour into well-greased and floured 9x13-inch baking pan. Bake at 325 degrees for 30 minutes. Cool slightly. Cut into bars.

Photograph for this recipe below.

HEAVENLY BROWNIES

⅔ c. shortening
5 oz. chocolate
1 c. sugar
2 eggs, beaten
1½ tsp. vanilla extract
1¼ c. flour
½ tsp. baking powder
1 tsp. salt
1 c. chopped walnuts
1 c. miniature marshmallows
2 tbsp. butter
3 tbsp. coffee
2 c. sifted confectioners' sugar

Melt shortening and 3 ounces chocolate in saucepan over low heat. Combine sugar and eggs in bowl; beat well. Stir in 1 teaspoon vanilla and chocolate mixture. Sift flour, baking powder and ½ teaspoon salt together. Add to chocolate mixture with walnuts; mix well. Pour into greased 9-inch round baking pan. Bake at 325 degrees for 25 minutes. Top hot brownies with marshmallows. Let stand until melted. Spread evenly over brownies. Melt butter and 2 ounces chocolate in saucepan over low heat. Add ½ teaspoon vanilla, ½ teaspoon salt and remaining ingredients. Beat until glossy. Spread over brownies. Cool. Cut into wedges.

Dede Speed, Oklahoma

GERMAN CHOCOLATE BROWNIES

1   4-oz. package German's sweet chocolate
5 tbsp. butter, softened
3 eggs
1 c. sugar
9 tbsp. flour
½ tsp. baking powder
¼ tsp. salt
1½ tsp. vanilla extract
½ c. chopped pecans
1   3-oz. package cream cheese, softened

Melt chocolate with 3 tablespoons butter in saucepan over low heat, stirring constantly. Cool. Beat 2 eggs in bowl until light. Add ¾ cup sugar gradually. Blend in mixture of ½ cup flour, baking powder and salt. Stir in chocolate mixture, 1 teaspoon vanilla and pecans. Cream 2 tablespoons butter, cream cheese and ¼ cup sugar in bowl. Blend in 1 egg, 1 tablespoon flour and ½ teaspoon vanilla. Layer half the chocolate batter, all the cream cheese mixture and remaining chocolate batter in greased 8-inch square baking pan. Cut with knife to marbleize. Bake at 350 degrees for 35 minutes or until brownies test done. Cool. Cut into squares.

Julie Wilczynski, California

HUNDRED-DOLLAR BROWNIES

1½ sticks butter
5 sq. bitter chocolate
2 c. sugar
5 eggs
1 c. sifted flour
½ tsp. salt
2½ tsp. vanilla extract
2¼ c. confectioners' sugar
1½ tsp. lemon juice
1 c. chopped pecans

Melt 1 stick butter and 4 squares chocolate over low heat in heavy saucepan. Cool. Stir in sugar. Add 4 eggs 1 at a time, mixing well after each addition. Add flour, salt and 1 teaspoon vanilla; mix well. Pour into greased and floured 10x15-inch baking pan. Bake at 350 degrees for 20 minutes or just until firm. Do not overbake. Melt ½ stick butter and 1 square chocolate over low heat in heavy saucepan. Stir in confectioners' sugar, blending well. Remove from heat. Add 1 egg; beat well. Add 1½ teaspoons vanilla and lemon juice; mix well. Stir in pecans. Add enough additional confectioners' sugar to make of spreading consistency. Spread frosting over warm brownies. Cool. Cut into squares.

Helen Exum, Tennessee

IRISH CREAM BROWNIES

3 oz. unsweetened baking chocolate
½ c. butter
1 c. sugar
2 eggs, well beaten
1 tbsp. Irish whiskey
⅔ c. flour
¼ tsp. salt
⅔ c. semisweet chocolate chips (opt.)
7 tbsp. Irish cream liqueur
1 c. confectioners' sugar
3 tbsp. butter, softened
Chopped nuts (opt.)

Melt chocolate with ½ cup butter in double boiler; mix well. Cool. Beat sugar with eggs in bowl. Add whiskey and cooled chocolate mixture; mix well. Stir in flour, salt and chocolate chips. Pour into buttered foil-lined 8x8-inch baking pan. Bake at 325 degrees for 20 minutes or until brownies test done. Cool for 2 hours or longer. Pierce with toothpick. Drizzle 3 tablespoons liqueur over brownies. Combine confectioners' sugar, 3 tablespoons butter and 4 tablespoons liqueur in bowl; mix well. Spread over brownies. Sprinkle with nuts. Cut into squares.

Shirley L. Warnock, California

HONEY BEAR BROWNIES

⅓ c. margarine, softened
¾ c. sugar
½ c. honey
2 tsp. vanilla extract
2 eggs
½ c. flour
⅓ c. cocoa
½ tsp. salt
1 c. chopped nuts

Cream margarine and sugar in bowl until light and fluffy. Blend in honey and vanilla. Add eggs 1 at a time, beating well after each addition. Combine flour, cocoa and salt. Add to creamed mixture gradually; mix well. Stir in nuts. Pour into greased 9x9-inch baking pan. Bake at 350 degrees for 25 minutes or until brownies test done. Cool. Cut into squares.

Carrie Waters, Ohio

MICROWAVE BROWNIES

⅔ c. butter
1 c. sugar
2 eggs
1 tsp. vanilla extract
1 c. flour
½ tsp. baking powder
½ tsp. salt
5 tbsp. cocoa
1 c. chopped pecans

Microwave butter in glass bowl on High until melted. Stir in sugar. Cool. Add eggs, vanilla and 2 tablespoons water; mix well. Add combined dry ingredients; mix well. Stir in pecans. Spread in greased 7x12-inch glass baking dish. Microwave on High for 6 to 7 minutes, turning 2 or 3 times. Cool. Cut into squares.

Linnette Padgett, Florida

MICROWAVE KAHLUA BROWNIES

½ c. butter
1 c. sugar
½ tsp. salt
3 tbsp. Kahlua
2 eggs
¾ c. flour
½ c. cocoa
1 c. chopped nuts (opt.)

Microwave butter in glass bowl on High for 1 minute. Add sugar, salt, Kahlua and eggs; beat well. Add mixture of flour, cocoa and nuts; mix well. Spread in greased 8-inch square glass baking dish. Microwave

on Medium-High for 16 minutes, turning ¼ turn every 4 minutes. Cool. Cut into squares. Store in refrigerator.
Note: Delicious when served with coffee ice cream topped with Kahlua and whipped cream.

Doris J. Gentry, California

MINI-CHIP BROWNIES

½ c. melted butter
1 c. packed light brown sugar
1 egg
1 tsp. vanilla extract
1 c. flour
½ tsp. salt
1 c. Hershey's miniature chocolate chips

Combine butter, brown sugar, egg and vanilla in mixer bowl. Beat until light and fluffy. Add mixture of flour and salt; mix until just blended. Stir in chocolate chips. Pour into greased 9-inch square baking dish. Bake at 350 degrees for 25 minutes or until brownies test almost done.

Photograph for this recipe on page 2.

MOCHA BRAN BROWNIES

1 6-oz. package semisweet chocolate chips
½ c. margarine
½ c. sugar
2 eggs
1½ tsp. vanilla extract
½ c. Kellogg's All-Bran
¾ c. flour
¼ tsp. soda
½ tsp. salt
2 tbsp. plus ½ tsp. instant coffee powder
½ c. chopped nuts
1 tbsp. milk
1 tbsp. margarine, softened
1 c. sifted confectioners' sugar

Melt chocolate chips and margarine in saucepan over very low heat, stirring frequently. Stir in sugar; remove from heat. Add eggs and 1 teaspoon vanilla; mix well. Mix cereal with ⅓ cup water. Let stand for 1 minute. Add to chocolate mixture with mixture of flour, soda, salt and 2 tablespoons coffee powder; mix well. Stir in nuts. Spread in greased 8-inch square baking pan. Bake at 350 degrees for 30 minutes or until toothpick inserted in center comes out clean. Cool. Dissolve ½ teaspoon coffee powder in milk in small mixer bowl. Add ½ teaspoon vanilla, softened margarine and confectioners' sugar. Beat until smooth. Spread over baked layer. Decorate with additional nuts. Cut into squares.

Photograph for this recipe on page 6.

PEANUTTY BROWNIE BARS

    ¾ c. melted butter
    ½ c. cocoa
    1¾ c. sugar
    1½ tsp. vanilla extract
    3 eggs
    1¼ c. flour
    ¼ tsp. baking powder
    1 c. peanut butter chips
    ⅓ c. semisweet chocolate chips
    1 tsp. shortening

Combine butter and cocoa in bowl; mix well. Add 1½ cups sugar and vanilla; mix well. Add eggs 1 at a time, mixing well after each addition. Stir in flour and baking powder. Spread in 10x15-inch baking pan lined with greased foil. Bake at 350 degrees for 14 minutes. Cool for 2 minutes. Invert onto wire rack. Peel off foil. Invert onto wire rack to cool completely. Combine ¼ cup sugar and ¼ cup water in saucepan. Bring to a boil. Remove from heat. Add peanut butter chips. Stir until chips melt. Cool slightly. Cut baked layer in half. Spread peanut butter mixture between and on top of layers. Let stand until set. Melt chocolate chips and shortening in double boiler over hot water; mix well. Drizzle over layers. Let stand until set. Cut into bars.

Photograph for this recipe on page 36.

ROCKY ROAD BROWNIES

    1 pkg. brownie mix
    2 c. miniature marshmallows
    1   6-oz. package semisweet chocolate chips
    ¼ c. milk
    ½ c. coarsely chopped nuts

Prepare and bake brownie mix using package directions. Sprinkle marshmallows over hot brownies. Combine chocolate chips and milk in saucepan. Cook until smooth, stirring constantly. Drizzle over brownies. Sprinkle with nuts. Cool. Cut into squares.

Amy Haynes, Georgia

ORANGE BROWNIES

    6 tbsp. margarine
    1 c. packed brown sugar
    ½ c. applesauce
    1 egg, beaten
    1 tsp. grated orange rind
    1½ tsp. vanilla extract
    1¼ c. flour
    1 tsp. baking powder
    ¼ tsp. soda
    ½ tsp. salt
    ½ c. chopped pecans
    1½ c. confectioners' sugar
    2 tbsp. orange juice

Combine margarine and brown sugar in saucepan. Heat until well blended, stirring constantly. Combine with applesauce, egg, orange rind and 1 teaspoon vanilla in bowl. Add mixture of flour, baking powder, soda and salt; mix well. Stir in pecans. Pour into greased and floured 7x12-inch baking pan. Bake at 350 degrees for 25 minutes. Combine confectioners' sugar, orange juice and ½ teaspoon vanilla in bowl; mix well. Spread over warm brownies. Cool. Cut into squares.

Erin Balzano, New Mexico

PRALINE-TOPPED BROWNIES

    ¾ c. butter, softened
    1 c. sugar
    2 eggs
    ½ tsp. vanilla extract
    2 oz. unsweetened chocolate, melted
    ¾ c. sifted flour
    ½ tsp. salt
    1 c. finely chopped pecans
    ½ c. packed brown sugar
    2 tbsp. cream

Cream ½ cup butter and sugar in bowl until light and fluffy. Add eggs 1 at a time, beating well after each addition. Blend in vanilla and chocolate. Sift in flour and salt; mix well. Fold in ½ cup pecans. Pour into greased 8-inch square baking pan. Bake at 450 degrees for 30 to 35 minutes. Cream brown sugar and remaining ¼ cup butter in bowl until light and fluffy. Blend in cream. Stir in remaining ½ cup pecans. Spread over hot brownies. Broil until topping is bubbly. Cut into squares while warm. Remove from pan to wire rack to cool.

Louise Whitlock, Arizona

SAUCEPAN BROWNIES

    ½ c. sugar
    2 tbsp. butter
    1⅓ c. Hershey's miniature chocolate chips
    2 eggs
    ⅔ c. flour
    ¼ tsp. each soda, salt
    1 tsp. vanilla extract
    ¾ c. chopped nuts (opt.)
    Confectioners' sugar

Combine sugar, butter and 2 tablespoons water in saucepan. Bring to a boil over medium heat, stirring occasionally. Add chocolate chips; stir until melted. Cool. Add eggs; mix well. Mix flour, soda and salt in bowl. Add chocolate mixture; mix well. Fold in vanilla and nuts. Pour into greased 9-inch square baking dish. Bake at 325 degrees for 25 to 30 minutes or until brownies test almost done. Cool. Sprinkle with confectioners' sugar. Cut into squares.

Photograph for this recipe on page 2.

ZUCCHINI BROWNIES

1/3 c. margarine
1 c. packed brown sugar
1 egg
1 tsp. vanilla extract
1 c. flour
1 tsp. baking powder
1/8 tsp. soda
1/2 tsp. salt
3/4 c. finely chopped zucchini
1/2 c. chopped pecans
1/4 c. butterscotch chips

Melt margarine with 1 tablespoon water in saucepan. Stir in brown sugar. Cool. Add egg; mix well. Add vanilla and dry ingredients; mix well. Stir in zucchini, pecans and butterscotch chips. Spread in greased and floured 9-inch square baking pan. Bake at 350 degrees for 20 minutes or until brownies test done. Cool. Cut into squares.

Thelma Brammer, West Virginia

CAROB BARS

1 1/2 sticks butter, melted
1 c. packed brown sugar
1/2 c. raw honey
3 eggs
1/4 c. oil
2 2/3 c. whole wheat flour
Dash of salt
1 tsp. baking powder
1/2 c. chopped pecans
1/2 c. flaked coconut
1 6-oz. package carob chips
1 tsp. vanilla extract

Combine butter and brown sugar in bowl; mix well. Add honey in fine stream, beating constantly. Add eggs 1 at a time, mixing well after each addition. Stir in oil, dry ingredients, pecans, coconut, carob chips and vanilla in order listed. Pour into greased

9x13-inch baking pan. Bake at 325 degrees for 20 minutes or until set. Cut into bars. Serve warm.

Tami L. Lewis, North Carolina

CARROT BARS

1/2 c. sugar
1/2 c. packed brown sugar
1/3 c. oil
1 tsp. cinnamon
2 eggs
2 1/2 c. buttermilk baking mix
3/4 c. finely shredded carrots
1/3 c. golden raisins
1 1/4 c. pecan halves
1 3-oz. package cream cheese, softened
1/4 c. confectioners' sugar
1 tbsp. butter, softened
1/4 tsp. vanilla extract

Combine sugars, oil, cinnamon, eggs and buttermilk baking mix in bowl. Beat just until blended. Stir in carrots and raisins. Reserve 60 pecan halves; chop remaining pecans. Add chopped pecans to batter; mix well. Spread in greased and floured 10x15-inch baking pan. Bake at 350 degrees for 20 minutes or until set. Cool in pan on wire rack. Cut into 5 lengthwise strips. Cut each strip crosswise into 12 strips. Combine remaining ingredients in bowl. Beat until smooth. Spoon into pastry bag fitted with large ribbon tip. Pipe frosting down center of each bar. Top each with reserved pecan half. Yield: 5 dozen.

Jan Rodgers, Tennessee

CHEESECAKE COOKIES

1/3 c. butter, softened
1/3 c. packed brown sugar
1 c. flour
1/2 c. chopped nuts
1 8-oz. package cream cheese, softened
1/4 c. sugar
1 egg
2 tbsp. milk
1 tbsp. lemon juice
1/2 tsp. vanilla extract

Cream butter and brown sugar in bowl until light and fluffy. Add flour and nuts; mix well. Reserve 1 cup for topping. Press remaining mixture into greased 8-inch square baking pan. Bake at 350 degrees for 12 minutes. Combine remaining ingredients in bowl; mix well. Pour over baked layer. Top with reserved nut mixture. Bake at 350 degrees for 30 minutes or until set. Cool. Cut into squares.

Monica Reilley, Illinois

CARAMEL-CHOCOLATE SQUARES

1   14-oz. package light caramels
⅓ c. evaporated milk
1   2-layer pkg. German chocolate cake mix
½ c. butter, softened
1 c. chopped nuts
1   6-oz. package semisweet chocolate chips

Combine caramels and evaporated milk in heavy saucepan. Cook over low heat until caramels are melted, stirring constantly. Keep warm. Combine cake mix, butter, nuts and 1 tablespoon water in bowl. Stir with fork until crumbly. Press half the mixture into greased and floured 9x13-inch baking pan. Bake at 350 degrees for 6 minutes. Sprinkle with chocolate chips. Spread with melted caramels. Sprinkle with remaining nut mixture. Bake at 350 degrees for 15 minutes. Cool. Cut into squares.

Christina Pitsch, Wisconsin

CASHEW DROPS

½ c. butter, softened
1 c. packed brown sugar
1 egg
1½ tsp. vanilla extract
2 c. flour
¾ tsp. each soda, baking powder
½ tsp. cinnamon
¼ tsp. each salt, nutmeg
⅓ c. sour cream
1 c. chopped cashews
3 tbsp. butter
2 tbsp. milk
2 c. sifted confectioners' sugar

Cream softened butter and brown sugar in bowl until light and fluffy. Add egg and ½ teaspoon vanilla; beat well. Combine flour, soda, baking powder, cinnamon, salt and nutmeg. Add to creamed mixture alternately with sour cream, mixing well after each addition. Stir in cashews. Drop by teaspoonfuls onto greased cookie sheet. Bake at 400 degrees for 8 minutes. Cool on wire rack. Brown 3 tablespoons butter in saucepan. Add 1 teaspoon vanilla, milk and confectioners' sugar; beat until smooth. Spread over cooled cookies. Yield: 4 dozen.

Gayla Carson, Virginia

CARDAMOM COOKIES

1 c. butter, softened
1 c. sugar
½ c. sour cream
4 c. sifted flour
¼ tsp. each salt, soda
1 tbsp. cardamom

Cream butter and sugar in bowl until light and fluffy. Add sour cream, flour, salt, soda and cardamom; mix well. Shape into two 2-inch diameter rolls. Wrap in plastic wrap. Chill overnight. Cut into ⅛-inch slices. Arrange on ungreased cookie sheet. Bake at 375 degrees for 8 minutes or until light brown. Cool on wire rack. Yield: 10 dozen.

Marge Brucker, Ohio

BROWN-EYED SUSAN COOKIES

1½ c. buttermilk baking mix
2 sm. packages vanilla instant pudding mix
2 eggs
¼ c. melted butter
42 milk chocolate candy stars

Mix baking mix and pudding mix in bowl. Add eggs and butter; mix well. Drop by teaspoonfuls onto ungreased cookie sheet. Bake at 350 degrees for 10 minutes or until light brown. Press candy star into center of each hot cookie. Cool on wire rack. Yield: 3½ dozen.

Kathy Blount, Alabama

CHERRY BARS

1¼ c. flour
1¼ c. confectioners' sugar
½ c. margarine, softened
¾ c. sugar
½ tsp. baking powder
Pinch of salt
2 eggs, beaten
½ c. chopped nuts
½ c. chopped maraschino cherries
½ c. coconut
Maraschino cherry juice

Mix 1 cup flour and ¼ cup confectioners' sugar in bowl. Cut in margarine until crumbly. Press into ungreased 8x8-inch baking pan. Bake at 350 degrees for 10 minutes. Combine ¼ cup flour, sugar, baking powder and salt in bowl. Blend in eggs. Stir in nuts, cherries and coconut. Spread over crust. Bake for 30 minutes. Blend 1 cup confectioners' sugar with a small amount of cherry juice. Spread over hot baked layer. Cool. Cut into bars.

Pat Duncan, Texas

CHERRY SWIRLS

1½ c. sugar
½ c. margarine, softened
½ c. shortening
4 eggs
1 tsp. each vanilla, almond extract
3 c. flour
1½ tsp. baking powder
1 can cherry pie filling
¾ c. confectioners' sugar
1 to 2 tbsp. milk

Cream sugar, margarine, shortening, eggs and flavorings in large mixer bowl. Beat at high speed for 3 minutes. Stir in flour and baking powder. Stir in flour and baking powder. Spread ⅔ of the batter on greased shallow baking sheet. Spread pie filling over batter. Bake at 350 degrees for 45 minutes. Blend confectioners' sugar with a small amount of milk. Drizzle over warm cake. Cool. Cut into squares.

Nancy Finck, Vermont

CHERRY-CHOCOLATE COOKIES

⅔ c. butter, softened
¾ c. plus 2 tbsp. sugar
1 egg
1½ tsp. vanilla extract
1⅔ c. flour
6 tbsp. cocoa
¼ tsp. each baking powder, soda
⅛ tsp. salt
36 maraschino cherry halves
½ c. semisweet chocolate chips

Cream butter, ¾ cup sugar, egg and vanilla in bowl until light and fluffy. Add mixture of flour, cocoa, baking powder, soda and salt; mix well. Shape into 1-inch balls. Place 1 inch apart on ungreased cookie sheet. Press cherry half into center of each cookie. Bake at 350 degrees for 8 minutes or until almost set. Cool on wire rack. Combine 2 tablespoons sugar and 2 tablespoons water in saucepan. Cook over medium heat until sugar dissolves. Remove from heat. Add chocolate chips. Stir until chocolate melts. Frost tops of cookies, leaving cherries unfrosted. Yield: 3 dozen.

Photograph for this recipe on page 36.

CHOCOLATE-COVERED CHERRY COOKIES

½ c. butter, softened
1 c. sugar
1 egg
1½ tsp. vanilla extract
1½ c. flour
½ c. cocoa
¼ tsp. each salt, soda and baking powder
36 maraschino cherries, drained
1 6-oz. package semisweet chocolate chips, melted
½ c. sweetened condensed milk
2 tsp. maraschino cherry juice

Cream butter, sugar, egg and vanilla in mixer bowl until light and fluffy. Add mixture of flour, cocoa, salt, soda and baking powder. Shape into 1-inch balls. Place on lightly greased cookie sheet. Press cherry firmly into each ball. Combine melted chocolate, condensed milk and cherry juice in bowl; blend well. Top each cookie with ½ teaspoon chocolate mixture. Bake at 350 degrees for 8 minutes or until firm. Cool on wire rack. Yield: 3 dozen.

Daniel Williams, Texas

◆◆◆◆◆◆◆◆◆◆◆◆◆◆◆◆◆◆◆◆◆◆◆◆◆◆◆◆◆◆

Hint: To shape easily, chill soft cookie dough.

◆◆◆◆◆◆◆◆◆◆◆◆◆◆◆◆◆◆◆◆◆◆◆◆◆◆◆◆◆◆

CHOCOLATE KISS COOKIES

½ c. butter, softened
1 c. sugar
1 egg
2 tsp. vanilla extract
1½ c. flour
⅓ c. cocoa
½ tsp. soda
¼ tsp. salt
6 tbsp. milk
1½ c. confectioners' sugar
1 tbsp. shortening
36 milk chocolate kisses

Cream butter, sugar, egg and 1½ teaspoons vanilla in bowl until light and fluffy. Add mixture of flour, cocoa, soda and salt alternately with ¼ cup milk, mixing well after each addition. Chill for 20 minutes. Shape into 1-inch balls. Place on ungreased cookie sheet. Bake at 375 degrees for 10 minutes. Cool for 1 minute. Combine ½ teaspoon vanilla, 2 tablespoons milk, confectioners' sugar and shortening in bowl; mix well. Spread on warm cookies, leaving ½-inch border. Place chocolate kiss in center of each cookie; press lightly. Cool on wire rack. Yield: 3 dozen.

Photograph for this recipe on page 1.

CHOCOLATE BALLS

1 c. shortening
1¼ c. confectioners' sugar
9 oz. German's chocolate, grated
1 c. chopped peanuts
2¼ c. flour
Vanilla extract to taste
1 c. sugar

Cream shortening and confectioners' sugar in bowl until light and fluffy. Add chocolate, peanuts, flour and vanilla; mix well. Shape into small balls. Place on ungreased cookie sheet. Bake at 250 degrees for 1 hour. Roll warm cookies in sugar. Cool. Yield: 6 dozen.

Barbara Reynolds, Maryland

CHOCOLATE-FILLED COOKIES

1¼ c. shortening
1 c. sugar
1 egg
2 c. flour
½ c. cocoa
½ tsp. soda
1 tsp. salt
1 c. milk
1 tbsp. vanilla extract
1 c. confectioners' sugar
1 c. marshmallow creme

Cream ½ cup shortening and sugar in large bowl until light and fluffy. Add egg; mix well. Sift flour, cocoa, soda and salt together. Add to creamed mixture alternately with milk and 1 teaspoon vanilla, mixing well after each addition. Drop by tablespoonfuls onto ungreased cookie sheet. Bake at 425 degrees for 5 minutes or until set. Cool on wire rack. Combine ¾ cup shortening, confectioners' sugar, marshmallow creme and 2 teaspoons vanilla in bowl; beat until fluffy. Spread filling over half the cookies; top with remaining cookies. Yield: 1½ dozen.

Wendi McGlothlin, Texas

CHOCOLATE THUMBPRINT COOKIES

½ c. plus 1 tbsp. butter, softened
⅔ c. plus 2 tbsp. sugar
1 egg, separated
¼ c. milk
1¼ tsp. vanilla extract
1 c. flour
¼ c. cocoa
¼ tsp. salt
1 c. finely chopped nuts

½ c. confectioners' sugar
Candied cherries (opt.)
Walnut or pecan halves (opt.)
Milk chocolate kisses (opt.)

Cream ½ cup butter, ⅔ cup sugar, egg yolk, 2 tablespoons milk and 1 teaspoon vanilla in bowl until light and fluffy. Add mixture of flour, cocoa and salt; blend well. Chill for 1 hour. Shape into 1-inch balls. Dip into beaten egg white. Coat with mixture of chopped nuts and 2 tablespoons sugar. Place on lightly greased cookie sheet. Make indentation in center of each. Bake at 350 degrees for 10 minutes or until set. Combine confectioners' sugar, 1 tablespoon butter, 2 tablespoons milk and ¼ teaspoon vanilla in bowl; mix well. Spoon ¼ teaspoon into each hot cookie. Place cherry, nut half or chocolate kiss in center. Cool on wire rack. Yield: 2 dozen.

Photograph for this recipe on page 53.

CHOCOLATE-PECAN CLUSTERS

¼ c. butter, softened
½ c. sugar
1 egg
1½ tsp. vanilla extract
1½ sq. unsweetened chocolate, melted
½ c. flour
¼ tsp. baking powder
½ tsp. salt
2 c. pecans

Cream butter and sugar in bowl until light and fluffy. Stir in egg and vanilla. Add chocolate and sifted dry ingredients; mix well. Stir in pecans. Drop by teaspoonfuls 1 inch apart on ungreased cookie sheet. Bake at 350 degrees for 10 minutes. Cool on wire rack. Yield: 3 dozen.

Margaret J. Sloan, Texas

COCOA CRUMB COOKIES

¼ c. butter, softened
½ c. sugar
¼ c. cocoa
2 eggs
1 tsp. vanilla extract
1 c. fine bread crumbs
Jam or jelly

Cream butter, sugar and cocoa in bowl until light and fluffy. Add eggs and vanilla; mix well. Stir in crumbs. Spread in greased 8-inch square baking pan. Bake at 300 degrees for 20 minutes. Cool. Cut into squares. Spread half the cookies with jam. Top with remaining cookies. Frost with chocolate frosting if desired. Yield: 2 dozen.

Jane D. Speight, Virginia

FILLED CHOCOLATE BARS

½ c. plus 2 tbsp. butter
2 oz. unsweetened baking chocolate
2 eggs, beaten
1¼ c. sugar
½ c. flour
¼ tsp. salt
1½ tsp. vanilla extract
1 c. finely chopped nuts
½ c. chocolate Mini Chips
1 c. confectioners' sugar
1 tbsp. milk
Sliced almonds or walnut halves

Melt ½ cup butter in saucepan. Remove from heat. Add baking chocolate; stir until melted. Combine eggs, 1 cup sugar, flour and salt in bowl; beat well. Add melted chocolate and 1 teaspoon vanilla; blend well. Stir in chopped nuts. Spread batter in greased waxed paper-lined 10x15-inch baking pan. Bake at 400 degrees for 10 minutes. Cool. Cut in half crosswise. Turn onto cutting board. Bring remaining ¼ cup sugar and 2 tablespoons water to a boil in saucepan. Add chocolate chips. Remove from heat. Stir until blended. Spread over 1 layer. Combine confectioners' sugar, milk, remaining 2 tablespoons butter and ½ teaspoon vanilla in bowl. Beat until smooth. Spread over remaining layer. Place chocolate-glazed layer on top. Cut into bars. Decorate with almonds or walnuts.

Photograph for this recipe on page 53.

CONGO SQUARES

⅔ c. melted margarine
2½ c. packed brown sugar
3 eggs
2¾ c. self-rising flour
1 c. finely chopped nuts
1 6-oz. package chocolate chips

Combine margarine and brown sugar in bowl; mix well. Add eggs 1 at a time, beating well after each addition. Stir in flour, nuts and chocolate chips. Pour into greased 9x13-inch baking pan. Bake at 350 degrees for 30 minutes. Cool. Cut into squares.

Scott Wilson, North Carolina

ROCKY ROAD DROPS

½ c. butter, softened
⅔ c. packed brown sugar
2 tsp. vanilla extract
1 egg, beaten

1 6-oz. package semisweet
chocolate chips, melted
½ c. chopped walnuts
⅓ c. milk
1½ c. sifted flour
½ tsp. soda
¾ tsp. salt
1 tsp. instant coffee powder
12 lg. marshmallows, sliced into thirds
36 California walnut halves
¼ c. melted butter
⅓ c. light cream
2½ c. sifted confectioners' sugar

Cream softened butter, brown sugar and 1 teaspoon vanilla in bowl until light and fluffy. Beat in egg. Add half the chocolate and chopped walnuts; mix well. Add milk and sifted flour, soda, salt and coffee powder; mix well. Drop by teaspoonfuls onto greased cookie sheet. Bake at 350 degrees for 10 minutes. Do not overbake; cookies should be moist. Top hot cookies with marshmallow slices. Bake for 1 minute longer. Remove to wire rack. Press walnut half into each marshmallow. Blend melted butter with cream and remaining chocolate in bowl. Add 1 teaspoon vanilla and confectioners' sugar; beat until smooth. Spoon warm frosting over slightly warm cookies. Yield: 3 dozen.

Photograph for this recipe below.

BANANA-CHOCOLATE CHIP COOKIES

1 c. sifted flour
1 tsp. baking powder
1 tsp. soda
¼ tsp. salt
⅓ c. margarine, softened
½ c. sugar
1 egg
½ c. mashed banana
1 6-oz. package chocolate chips
½ tsp. vanilla extract

Sift first 4 ingredients together. Cream margarine in bowl. Add sugar gradually, beating until light and fluffy. Add egg; mix well. Add flour mixture alternately with banana, beating until well blended after each addition. Stir in chocolate chips and vanilla. Drop by teaspoonfuls onto greased cookie sheet. Bake at 375 degrees for 10 minutes or until golden brown. Cool on wire rack. Yield: 3 dozen.

Alice M. Cook, Wisconsin

COCONUT-CHOCOLATE CHIP BARS

1 pkg. fluffy white frosting mix
1 tsp. vanilla extract
1 c. graham cracker crumbs
1 6-oz. package chocolate chips
½ c. flaked coconut
½ c. chopped pecans

Prepare frosting mix according to package directions, adding vanilla. Fold in remaining ingredients. Pour into greased 9-inch square baking pan. Bake at 350 degrees for 30 minutes. Cool. Cut into bars.

Marla Cail, Oklahoma

CINNAMON-CHIP COOKIES

2 c. flour
1 c. sugar
1 tsp. baking powder
1 tbsp. cinnamon
½ c. butter, softened
½ c. shortening
1 egg, separated
1 6-oz. package semisweet chocolate chips
½ c. chopped pecans
Cinnamon-sugar

Sift first 4 ingredients into bowl. Cut in butter and shortening until crumbly. Add beaten egg yolk; mix well. Stir in chocolate chips and pecans. Shape into 1-inch balls. Dip into beaten egg white; roll in cinnamon-sugar. Place on greased cookie sheet. Bake

at 350 degrees for 15 to 20 minutes or until puffed and golden brown.

Jan Hatfill, Florida

CHIPPED CHOCOLATE COOKIES

½ c. butter, softened
⅓ c. sugar
⅓ c. packed brown sugar
1 egg
½ tsp. vanilla extract
1¼ c. flour
½ tsp. soda
¼ tsp. salt
2 4-oz. packages sweet cooking chocolate, coarsely chipped
½ c. chopped walnuts

Cream butter and sugars in bowl until light and fluffy. Add egg, 1 tablespoon water and vanilla; mix well. Stir in mixture of flour, soda and salt. Fold in chocolate and walnuts. Drop by teaspoonfuls onto greased cookie sheet. Bake at 350 degrees for 15 minutes. Cool on wire rack. Yield: 3½ dozen.

Ellie Waterfield, Kansas

CHOW MEIN-CHIP COOKIES

2 sticks margarine, softened
½ c. sugar
1½ c. packed brown sugar
2 eggs
1½ tsp. vanilla extract
2 c. flour
1 tsp. soda
½ tsp. salt
2 c. quick-cooking oats
1 12-oz. package chocolate chips
2 c. chow mein noodles

Cream margarine and sugars in bowl until light and fluffy. Add eggs and vanilla; mix well. Add flour, soda and salt; mix well. Stir in oats, chocolate chips and noodles. Drop by teaspoonfuls onto ungreased cookie sheet. Bake at 350 degrees for 15 minutes. Cool on wire rack. Yield: 7 dozen.

Michelle Testerman, Virginia

CHOCOLATE CHIP COOKIES

⅔ c. shortening
⅔ c. butter, softened
1 c. sugar
1 c. packed brown sugar

2 eggs
2 tsp. vanilla extract
3 c. flour
1 tsp. each soda, salt
1 c. chopped nuts
1   12-oz. package chocolate chips

Cream first 6 ingredients in bowl until light and fluffy. Add mixture of flour, soda and salt; mix well. Stir in nuts and chocolate chips. Drop by teaspoonfuls onto ungreased cookie sheet. Bake at 375 degrees for 8 minutes or until light brown. Yield: 7 dozen.

Ginny Barefoot, Oklahoma

MINI-CHIP DROPS

¼ c. butter, softened
⅔ c. sugar
1 egg
1½ tsp. vanilla extract
1 c. miniature chocolate chips, melted
½ c. flour
¼ tsp. baking powder
¼ tsp. salt
1 c. miniature chocolate chips
½ c. chopped nuts

Cream butter and sugar in mixer bowl until light and fluffy. Add egg and vanilla. Blend in melted chocolate. Add mixture of flour, baking powder and salt; mix well. Stir in 1 cup chocolate chips and nuts. Drop by rounded teaspoonfuls onto ungreased cookie sheet. Bake at 350 degrees for 8 minutes or until set. Cool slightly on cookie sheet before removing to wire rack to cool completely. Yield: 2½ dozen.

Jason Thackrey, Indiana

MINT-CHOCOLATE CHIP COOKIES

8 sm. chocolate-covered mint patties
1 c. shortening
½ c. sugar
½ c. packed brown sugar
2 eggs
2 tsp. vanilla extract
2⅓ c. flour
1 tsp. each salt, soda
1   12-oz. package chocolate chips
½ c. chopped nuts

Melt mints in double boiler. Cream shortening, sugars, eggs and vanilla in large bowl until light and fluffy. Add mixture of flour, salt and soda; blend well. Stir in chocolate chips and nuts. Swirl in melted mints lightly. Drop by teaspoonfuls onto ungreased

cookie sheet. Bake at 350 degrees for 8 minutes or until golden brown. Cool on wire rack. Yield: 6 dozen.

Marci Ferkovich, Washington

PEANUT BUTTER-CHIP COOKIES

1 c. butter, softened
¾ c. packed brown sugar
¾ c. sugar
2 eggs
½ tsp. vanilla extract
2¼ c. flour
1 tsp. soda
½ tsp. salt
1 c. chocolate chips
1½ c. peanut butter chips

Cream first 5 ingredients in bowl until light and fluffy. Add mixture of flour, soda and salt; mix well. Stir in chocolate and peanut butter chips. Spread in greased 10x15-inch baking pan. Bake at 350 degrees for 25 minutes or until golden brown. Cool. Cut into bars.

Stacey Basham, Oklahoma

RAISIN-CHOCOLATE CHIP COOKIES

1 c. margarine, softened
¾ c. packed brown sugar
¾ c. sugar
1 tsp. vanilla extract
2 eggs
2½ c. sifted flour
1 tsp. soda
½ tsp. salt
2 c. raisins
1   12-oz. package semisweet
      chocolate chips

Combine margarine, sugars, vanilla, eggs and 1 teaspoon water in large mixer bowl; beat until creamy. Sift in flour, soda and salt; mix well. Stir in raisins and chocolate chips. Drop by teaspoonfuls 1½ inches apart onto greased cookie sheet. Bake at 375 degrees for 8 minutes. Cool on wire rack. Yield: 6 dozen.

Margaret Glover, Texas

◆◆◆◆◆◆◆◆◆◆◆◆◆◆◆◆◆◆◆◆◆◆◆◆◆◆◆◆

Hint: *To prevent cookies from sticking, use unsalted shortening for greasing baking pans and cookie sheets.*

◆◆◆◆◆◆◆◆◆◆◆◆◆◆◆◆◆◆◆◆◆◆◆◆◆◆◆◆

SUPER CHOCOLATE CHIP COOKIE

1 stick butter, softened
1/3 c. packed brown sugar
1/4 c. sugar
1 egg
1 tsp. vanilla extract
1 1/3 c. flour
1/2 tsp. soda
1/4 tsp. salt
1   6-oz. package semisweet chocolate
    chips
1/2 c. chopped nuts

Cream butter and sugars in large mixer bowl until light and fluffy. Add egg and vanilla, beating well after each addition. Beat in flour, soda and salt gradually at low speed. Fold in chocolate chips and nuts. Spread evenly in greased 13-inch round baking pan. Bake at 350 degrees for 15 minutes or until golden brown. Cut into wedges. Cool on wire rack.

Betty Woodall, Texas

CANDY CANE COOKIES

2 c. confectioners' sugar
1 c. butter, softened
1 c. shortening
2 eggs
1 tsp. almond extract
2 tsp. vanilla extract
5 c. flour
1/2 tsp. salt
1 tsp. red food coloring
1 c. sugar
1 c. crushed peppermint candy

Combine confectioners' sugar, butter, shortening, eggs and flavorings in bowl; blend well. Add flour and salt; mix well. Divide into 2 portions. Mix food coloring into 1 portion. Shape by teaspoonfuls into 4-inch ropes. Twist 1 red and 1 white rope together; shape into cane on cookie sheet. Bake at 375 degrees for 9 minutes or until light brown. Sprinkle hot cookies with mixture of sugar and candy. Cool on wire rack. Yield: 8 dozen.

Kevin Black, Oklahoma

CHRISTMAS TREES

1 c. shortening
1   3-oz. package cream cheese, softened
1/2 c. sugar
1 tsp. vanilla extract
2 c. sifted flour
2 or 3 drops of green food coloring

Cream shortening, cream cheese, sugar and vanilla in bowl until light and fluffy. Add flour and food coloring; mix well. Fill cookie press fitted with tree plate. Press cookies onto ungreased cookie sheet. Decorate as desired. Bake at 375 degrees for 6 minutes or until light brown. Cool on wire rack.
Yield: 4 dozen.

Diane Meier, Tennessee

CHRISTMAS BALL COOKIES

1 3/4 c. (about) flour
2/3 c. butter, softened
1 c. sugar
1 egg
1 egg, separated
1/4 tsp. salt
1/2 c. finely chopped walnuts
Cherry and mint jelly
2 tsp. vanilla extract

Sift flour 4 times. Measure 2 cups. Cream butter and 1/2 cup sugar in bowl until light and fluffy. Add 1 egg and 1 egg yolk. Stir in vanilla, salt and flour. Shape into small balls. Dip in beaten egg white. Roll in mixture of walnuts and 1/2 cup sugar. Place on lightly greased cookie sheet. Make small depression in each cookie. Fill with jelly. Bake at 300 degrees for 12 minutes or until brown. Cool on wire rack.
Yield: 5 dozen.

Diane Elder, California

CHRISTMAS PEPPERNUTS

1 1/2 c. sugar
1/2 c. margarine, softened
2 eggs
2 tbsp. sour milk
1 tsp. each cinnamon, cloves and nutmeg
1 tsp. soda
2 1/2 c. flour
1 c. finely chopped raisins
1/2 c. finely chopped nuts
1/2 c. shredded coconut

Cream sugar and margarine in bowl until light and fluffy. Add eggs and sour milk. Add mixture of spices, soda and flour; mix well. Stir in raisins, nuts and coconut. Chill overnight. Shape into 1/2-inch ropes. Cut into thin slices. Place on greased cookie sheet. Bake at 350 degrees until brown. Cool on foil-lined surface. Store in airtight container.

Mary Funk, Texas

HOLIDAY FRUITCAKE BARS

1   6-oz. can frozen orange juice
      concentrate, thawed
½ c. packed light brown sugar
1 c. raisins
1   8-oz. package dates, chopped
1   16-oz. jar mixed candied fruit,
      finely chopped
½ c. butter, softened
⅔ c. packed brown sugar
4 eggs
1 c. flour
Pinch of soda
½ tsp. each cinnamon, nutmeg
¼ tsp. each allspice, cloves
1 c. chopped nuts
1½ c. sifted confectioners' sugar
1 tbsp. butter
¼ c. orange juice

Combine orange juice concentrate and light brown sugar in medium saucepan. Bring to a boil over low heat, stirring constantly. Add raisins and dates. Bring to a boil; remove from heat. Stir in candied fruit. Set aside. Cream ½ cup butter and ⅔ cup brown sugar in large bowl. Add eggs 1 at a time, mixing well after each addition. Add dry ingredients except confectioners' sugar; mix well. Stir in nuts and fruit mixture. Spread in 2 waxed paper-lined 10x15-inch baking pans. Bake at 300 degrees for 35 minutes or until cake tests done. Cool. Mix confectioners' sugar, 1 tablespoon butter and orange juice in small bowl. Frost baked layers. Cut into bars. Garnish with candied cherry halves.

Jennifer Ellis, California

TUTTI-FRUTTI BARS

½ c. butter, softened
¾ c. packed brown sugar
1 egg
½ tsp. vanilla extract
1¼ c. flour
½ tsp. each soda, salt
1 c. mixed candied fruit
¾ c. semisweet chocolate chips
½ c. coarsely chopped nuts

Cream butter, brown sugar, egg and vanilla in bowl until light and fluffy. Add mixture of flour, soda and salt; mix well. Spread in greased 9x13-inch baking pan. Bake at 350 degrees for 12 minutes or until light brown. Cool. Spread with Vanilla Filling. Sprinkle fruit, chocolate chips and nuts over filling. Bake at 350 degrees for 15 minutes. Cool completely. Cut into bars.

Vanilla Filling

2 tbsp. sugar
2 tbsp. milk
1 tbsp. melted butter
½ tsp. vanilla extract
1 egg
⅓ c. flour
½ tsp. soda
¼ tsp. salt

Combine sugar, milk, butter, vanilla and egg in small mixer bowl. Beat until smooth. Add flour, soda and salt. Beat until blended.

Photograph for this recipe on page 36.

SANTA'S WHISKERS

1 c. butter, softened
1 c. sugar
2 tbsp. milk
1 tsp. vanilla extract
2½ c. flour
¾ c. finely chopped red candied cherries
½ c. finely chopped pecans
¾ c. flaked coconut

Cream butter and sugar in bowl until light and fluffy. Add milk and vanilla; mix well. Stir in flour, cherries and pecans. Shape into two 8-inch rolls. Coat with coconut; wrap in waxed paper. Chill until firm. Cut into ¼-inch slices. Place on greased cookie sheet. Bake at 375 degrees for 12 minutes or until edges are golden. Cool on wire rack. Yield: 5 dozen.

Tammy Jeffcoat, Oklahoma

CINNAMON SNOWBALLS

1 c. margarine, softened
⅓ c. sugar
2 tsp. vanilla extract
1¾ c. flour
1 tsp. cinnamon
¾ c. Kellogg's cornflake crumbs
1 c. finely chopped nuts
Confectioners' sugar, sifted

Cream margarine, sugar and vanilla in bowl until light and fluffy. Add mixture of flour, cinnamon, cornflake crumbs and nuts; mix well. Shape into ¾-inch balls; place on ungreased cookie sheet. Bake at 350 degrees for 15 minutes or until light brown. Roll warm cookies in confectioners' sugar. Cool. Re-roll in confectioners' sugar. Yield: 7 dozen.

Photograph for this recipe on page 6.

HOLIDATE MALT CHEWS

¾ c. packed brown sugar
6 tbsp. butter, melted
2 eggs, beaten
½ tsp. vanilla extract
¾ c. sifted flour
½ c. chocolate malted milk powder
½ tsp. baking powder
1 c. chopped dates
½ c. chopped walnuts
½ c. flaked coconut
2 tbsp. confectioners' sugar

Cream brown sugar and butter in large bowl until light and fluffy. Add eggs and vanilla; mix well. Add flour, malted milk powder and baking powder; mix well. Fold in dates, walnuts and coconut. Spread in greased and floured 9-inch square baking pan. Bake at 350 degrees for 25 minutes or until brown. Cool. Sprinkle with confectioners' sugar. Cut into squares.

Robert Long, Texas

HOLIDAY MINT BARS

½ c. butter, softened
1 c. sugar
2 eggs
1 tsp. vanilla extract
3   1-oz. squares unsweetened
    chocolate, melted
½ c. sifted flour
½ c. chopped nuts
1 c. confectioners' sugar
1 tbsp. cream
½ tsp. peppermint extract
Green food coloring
3 tbsp. butter, softened

Cream ½ cup butter and sugar in bowl until light and fluffy. Add eggs and vanilla. Blend in ⅔ of the chocolate. Stir in flour and nuts. Spoon batter into greased 8-inch square pan. Bake at 350 degrees for 25 minutes. Cool. Combine confectioners' sugar, cream, flavoring, food coloring and 2 tablespoons butter in small bowl. Beat until creamy. Spread mint frosting over brownies. Let stand until set. Combine remaining melted chocolate with 1 tablespoon melted butter. Spread chocolate glaze over frosting. Chill until firm. Cut into bars.

Dede Wallace, Texas

SNOWFLAKES

2 eggs, slightly beaten
2 tbsp. sugar
1 c. milk

1 c. sifted flour
¼ tsp. salt
1 tbsp. lemon extract
Oil for deep frying
2 to 3 c. confectioners' sugar

Combine eggs, sugar and milk in bowl; mix well. Sift in flour and salt; beat until smooth. Stir in flavoring. Chill, covered, for 2 hours. Heat oil in saucepan to 375 degrees. Dip rosette iron into batter. Do not coat completely. Dip iron into hot oil. Cook for 30 seconds. Loosen rosette with fork. Continue to cook until brown on both sides. Drain on paper towel. Coat hot rosette with confectioners' sugar. Repeat with remaining batter.
Yield: 5 dozen.

Kathleen Pickett, Louisiana

BUTTER BRANDY WREATHS

1⅓ c. butter, softened
¾ c. sugar
3 tbsp. Brandy
3¼ c. flour
Red cinnamon candies
Citron pieces

Cream butter and sugar in bowl until light and fluffy. Add Brandy; mix well. Add flour gradually; mix until smooth. Shape by teaspoonfuls into 8-inch ropes. Fold ends together; twist several times. Shape into ring on ungreased cookie sheet; seal ends. Decorate with candies and citron. Bake at 350 degrees for 10 minutes or until golden. Cool on wire rack.
Yield: 10 dozen.

Susan O'Connor, Tennessee

HOLIDAY WREATHS

1 c. butter
¾ c. confectioners' sugar
2 c. flour
½ tsp. salt
½ tsp. almond extract
1 c. quick-cooking oats
Red or green food coloring (opt.)
Red or green candied cherries, chopped

Cream butter and sugar in bowl until light and fluffy. Add flour, salt and almond extract; mix well. Stir in oats. Tint with food coloring. Shape by rounded teaspoonfuls into 6-inch ropes. Shape each rope on cookie sheet to form circle, overlapping ends. Decorate top of wreaths with candied cherry pieces. Bake at 350 degrees for 10 minutes. Cool on cookie sheet for 1 minute. Remove to wire rack to cool completely.
Yield: 3 dozen.

Marjorie Jerniggen, Tennessee

SHORTBREAD WREATHS

1 c. butter, softened
½ c. sugar
2 c. flour
1 tsp. vanilla extract
16 pecan halves
48 candied cherry halves
½ c. (about) confectioners' sugar

Cream butter and sugar in bowl until light and fluffy. Add flour and vanilla; mix until smooth. Chill for several hours. Shape into two 18-inch ropes. Arrange each in circle on ungreased cookie sheet. Pinch to join ends; flatten to ½-inch thickness. Decorate with pecans and cherries. Bake at 300 degrees for 30 minutes or until golden brown and crisp. Cool on baking sheet for 5 minutes before removing to wire rack to cool completely. Dust with confectioners' sugar. Cut into wedges. Yield: 2 dozen.

Judi Landry, Texas

HOLIDAY ZINGERS

1 stick margarine, softened
1½ c. packed brown sugar
4 eggs
4 c. flour
1 tbsp. soda
1 tsp. each nutmeg, cloves, cinnamon
  and allspice
2 lb. each candied cherries,
  pineapple, chopped
1 lb. dates, chopped
1 lb. white raisins
6 c. chopped pecans
1 c. pineapple juice

Cream margarine and brown sugar in large bowl until light and fluffy. Add eggs; mix well. Add mixture of dry ingredients alternately with fruit, pecans and pineapple juice, mixing well after each addition. Drop by teaspoonfuls onto greased cookie sheet. Bake at 325 degrees for 15 minutes or until brown. Cool on wire rack. Yield: 12 dozen.

Evelyn Mercer, West Virginia

NOEL COOKIE GEMS

½ c. shortening
¾ c. sugar
1 egg
1 tsp. vanilla extract
2⅔ c. flour
½ tsp. salt
¼ tsp. each baking powder, soda

½ c. sour cream
1¼ c. finely chopped pecans
½ c. preserves

Combine shortening, sugar, egg and vanilla in mixer bowl. Beat at medium speed until well blended. Add sifted dry ingredients alternately with sour cream, mixing well after each addition. Shape into 1¼-inch balls. Roll in pecans. Place 1 inch apart on greased baking sheet. Make indentation in center of each ball. Fill with preserves. Bake at 400 degrees for 10 minutes or until light brown. Cool on wire rack. Yield: 4½ dozen.

Vincent Scialo, California

SPRINKLE-TOP COOKIES

1 c. butter, softened
¾ c. sifted confectioners' sugar
1 tbsp. vanilla extract
2 c. flour
¾ tsp. salt
½ c. oats
½ c. semisweet chocolate chips
¼ c. milk
Finely chopped pecans, shredded coconut
  or chocolate shot

Cream butter, confectioners' sugar and vanilla in bowl. Stir in flour, salt and oats. Shape by teaspoonfuls into balls or crescents; place on ungreased cookie sheet. Bake at 325 degrees for 20 minutes or until light golden. Do not overbake. Cool on wire rack. Melt chocolate chips with milk; blend well. Dip cookie tops into melted chocolate then into pecans, coconut or chocolate shot. Yield: 4 dozen.

Vicki Dietz, New York

NORWEGIAN BUTTER KNOTS

4 eggs separated
1 c. sugar
½ c. sour cream
½ tsp. soda
1 tsp. vanilla or almond extract
Loaf sugar, coarsely crushed
1 c. butter, softened
4 c. flour

Beat egg yolks and 1 cup sugar in bowl. Add mixture of sour cream, soda and flavoring; mix well. Cut butter into flour in bowl until crumbly. Add sour cream mixture; mix well. Divide into small portions. Roll each into small rope; shape into wreath or knot. Dip into beaten egg white; coat with coarse sugar. Place on lightly greased cookie sheet. Bake at 350 degrees until golden. Cool on wire rack.

Carol Ludtke, Minnesota

COCONUT-CHERRY KISS COOKIES

⅓ c. butter, softened
1 3-oz. package cream cheese, softened
⅔ c. sugar
1 egg yolk
1 tsp. vanilla extract
1¼ c. flour
2 tsp. baking powder
¼ tsp. salt
½ c. chopped maraschino cherries
1 14-oz. package flaked coconut
1 9-oz. package milk chocolate kisses

Cream butter, cream cheese and sugar in bowl until light and fluffy. Add egg yolk and vanilla; beat well. Stir in mixture of flour, baking powder and salt gradually. Add cherries and 3 cups coconut; mix gently. Chill, tightly covered, for 1 hour. Shape into 1-inch balls. Roll in remaining coconut. Place on ungreased cookie sheet. Bake at 350 degrees for 10 minutes or until light brown. Remove from oven. Place chocolate kiss in center of each cookie; press lightly. Cool on cookie sheet for 1 minute. Cool completely on wire rack. Yield: 4½ dozen.

Photograph for this recipe on page 1.

COCONUT-CHERRY DROPS

½ c. butter, softened
½ c. sugar
1 egg
½ tsp. almond extract
1¼ c. flour
½ tsp. each baking powder, salt
1 c. flaked coconut
½ c. chopped pecans
¼ c. chopped maraschino cherries

Cream butter and sugar in bowl until light and fluffy. Add egg and flavoring; mix well. Add mixture of flour, baking powder and salt; mix well. Stir in remaining ingredients. Drop by teaspoonfuls onto greased cookie sheet. Bake at 375 degrees for 10 minutes or until light brown. Cool on wire rack. Yield: 3 dozen.

Lucy McCune, Pennsylvania

COCONUT CRUNCH COOKIES

1 c. shortening
1 c. packed brown sugar
½ c. sugar
2 eggs
2 tbsp. milk
1 tsp. vanilla extract
2 c. flour
1 tsp. each soda, salt
½ c. chopped walnuts
1 c. chopped chocolate-coated coconut
  candy bars

Cream shortening and sugars in bowl until light and fluffy. Add eggs, milk and vanilla; mix well. Add mixture of flour, soda and salt; mix well. Stir in walnuts and candy. Drop by tablespoonfuls 2 inches apart onto ungreased cookie sheet. Bake at 375 degrees for 10 minutes or until brown. Cool on wire rack. Yield: 4 dozen.

Note: Dough may be chilled, shaped into 1-inch balls and baked for 12 minutes.

Cindy Grey, Colorado

HONEY-GLAZED COCONUT BALLS

1 c. butter, softened
½ c. sugar
1 tsp. vanilla extract
1 tsp. almond extract
2 c. flour
1 c. chopped pecans
1 c. flaked coconut
¼ c. honey
¼ c. apricot preserves
1 tbsp. butter

Cream softened butter and sugar in bowl until light and fluffy. Blend in flavorings and flour. Add pecans and coconut; mix well. Chill for 1 hour. Shape by teaspoonfuls into balls; place on ungreased cookie sheet. Bake at 350 degrees for 15 minutes or until golden brown. Cool on wire rack. Combine honey, preserves and 1 tablespoon butter in saucepan. Bring to a simmer over low heat, stirring constantly. Simmer for 5 minutes. Dip each cookie into glaze; place on waxed paper. Let stand until set. Yield: 5 dozen.

Veda Pratt, Iowa

COCONUT SQUARES

6 tbsp. butter, softened
¼ c. sugar
¼ tsp. salt
1 c. flour
2 eggs, slightly beaten
1 tsp. vanilla extract
1 c. packed brown sugar
2 tbsp. flour
1 c. flaked coconut
½ c. chopped walnuts

Cream butter, sugar and salt in bowl until light and fluffy. Add 1 cup flour; mix well. Press into greased 9x9-inch baking pan. Bake at 350 degrees for 15 minutes. Mix eggs and vanilla in bowl. Beat in brown sugar and 2 tablespoons flour gradually. Stir in coconut and walnuts. Spread over baked layer. Bake at 350 degrees for 20 minutes or until toothpick inserted in center comes out clean. Cool. Cut into squares.

Brooke Lawson, Indiana

JAVA COCONUT COOKIES

½ c. butter, softened
1 c. packed brown sugar
1 egg
1 8-oz. carton sour cream
5 1-oz. envelopes premelted
unsweetened chocolate
2 c. flour
½ tsp. each soda, salt
1 tsp. instant coffee powder
1⅓ c. flaked coconut
2 c. (or more) confectioners' sugar

Cream butter and brown sugar in bowl until light and fluffy. Add egg, ⅔ cup sour cream and 3 envelopes chocolate; mix well. Add mixture of flour, soda, salt and coffee powder; mix well. Stir in half the coconut. Drop by teaspoonfuls onto greased cookie sheet. Bake at 375 degrees for 12 to 15 minutes. Combine 2 envelopes chocolate, remaining sour cream and enough confectioners' sugar to make of desired consistency. Spread over warm cookies; sprinkle with remaining coconut. Cool on wire rack. Yield: 4 dozen.

Kathy Charla, Michigan

CREAM CHEESE FRUITIES

¼ c. margarine, softened
1 8-oz. package cream cheese, softened
1 egg
1 tsp. vanilla extract
1 2-layer pkg. yellow cake mix
½ c. finely chopped pecans
½ c. finely chopped candied fruit

Cream margarine, cream cheese, egg and vanilla in mixer bowl until light and fluffy. Add cake mix. Beat until smooth. Stir in pecans and candied fruit. Drop by teaspoonfuls onto greased cookie sheet. Bake at 350 degrees for 8 minutes or until light brown. Cool on wire rack. Yield: 4 dozen.

Theodosia Blake, West Virginia

HUNGARIAN CREAM CHEESE KIFLIKS

3 c. sifted flour
1 8-oz. package cream cheese, softened
2 sticks margarine, softened
1 lb. walnuts, ground
1 tsp. cinnamon
⅓ c. sugar
1 jar raspberry jam
Confectioners' sugar

Combine first 3 ingredients in bowl; mix well. Shape into 1-inch balls. Chill, covered, overnight. Mix walnuts, cinnamon and sugar in bowl. Fold in jam. Roll each ball into circle on confectioners' sugar-covered surface. Place a small amount of jam mixture in center. Roll to enclose filling. Shape into crescents on ungreased cookie sheet. Bake at 350 degrees for 20 minutes or until golden. Place on wire rack. Cool. Sprinkle with confectioners' sugar. Yield: 4 dozen.

Beth Hemminger, Pennsylvania

◆◆◆◆◆◆◆◆◆◆◆◆◆◆◆◆◆◆◆◆◆◆◆◆◆◆◆◆◆◆

Hint: *To save cookie sheet clean-ups, shape cookies on sheets of waxed paper or foil and slide 1 at a time onto cookie sheet for baking.*

◆◆◆◆◆◆◆◆◆◆◆◆◆◆◆◆◆◆◆◆◆◆◆◆◆◆◆◆◆◆

COFFEE DROP COOKIES

1 c. shortening
2 c. packed light brown sugar
2 eggs
3 c. sifted flour
1 tbsp. baking powder
2 tsp. cinnamon
¼ tsp. salt
2 c. seedless raisins
1 c. cold strong coffee

Cream first 3 ingredients in large bowl until light and fluffy. Sift dry ingredients into bowl. Stir in raisins. Add to creamed mixture alternately with coffee, beating well after each addition. Drop by teaspoonfuls onto greased cookie sheet. Bake at 375 degrees for 12 minutes or until golden. Cool on wire rack. Yield: 6 dozen.

Dorothy A. Small, West Virginia

◆◆◆◆◆◆◆◆◆◆◆◆◆◆◆◆◆◆◆◆◆◆◆◆◆◆◆◆◆◆

Hint: *To promote even heat circulation, use cookie sheets at least 2 inches smaller than oven rack in each dimension.*

◆◆◆◆◆◆◆◆◆◆◆◆◆◆◆◆◆◆◆◆◆◆◆◆◆◆◆◆◆◆

CRACKERJACK COOKIES

1 c. butter, softened
1 c. sugar
1 c. packed brown sugar
2 eggs
2 tsp. vanilla extract
1½ c. flour
1 tsp. baking powder
1 tsp. soda
2 c. oats
1 c. flaked coconut
2 c. crisp rice cereal

Cream butter and sugars in bowl until light and fluffy. Add eggs and vanilla; beat until smooth. Stir in sifted dry ingredients, oats, coconut and cereal. Drop by teaspoonfuls onto greased cookie sheet. Bake at 350 degrees for 10 minutes. Cool on wire rack. Yield: 6 dozen.

Beverly Towler, Manitoba, Canada

CRANBERRY CRUNCH SQUARES

1 c. quick-cooking oats
½ c. flour
¾ c. packed brown sugar
½ c. coconut
⅓ c. margarine
1 16-oz. can whole cranberry sauce
1 tbsp. lemon juice

Combine oats, flour, brown sugar and coconut in bowl. Cut in margarine until crumbly. Press half the mixture into greased 8x8-inch baking pan. Mix cranberry sauce and lemon juice in bowl. Spread over crumb layer. Top with remaining oats mixture. Bake at 350 degrees for 30 minutes or until brown. Cool. Cut into squares. Serve with whipped cream or ice cream.

Mildred Anderson, Ohio

CURRANT COOKIES

4 c. flour
1½ c. sugar
1 tbsp. baking powder
¾ tsp. salt
1 tsp. nutmeg
1 c. shortening
¼ c. (about) milk
3 eggs, beaten
1 c. currants

Mix flour, sugar, baking powder, salt and nutmeg in bowl. Cut in shortening until crumbly. Add enough milk to eggs to measure 1 cup. Stir into flour mixture. Add currants; mix well. Chill in refrigerator. Roll on floured surface. Cut into circles. Bake on medium-hot griddle until brown on both sides. Cool on wire rack. Yield: 3 dozen.

Phyllis McNamara, Pennsylvania

CUSTARD SQUARES

½ c. margarine, softened
½ c. packed brown sugar
1⅓ c. flour
¼ tsp. salt
½ tsp. each cinnamon, ginger
¼ tsp. nutmeg
1 c. sour cream
1 egg
¼ c. sugar
½ tsp. soda
⅓ c. chopped nuts

Cream margarine and brown sugar in bowl until light and fluffy. Add mixture of flour, salt and spices; mix well. Reserve ½ cup for topping. Pat remaining mixture into greased 9-inch square baking pan. Bake at 350 degrees for 15 minutes. Combine sour cream, egg, sugar and soda in bowl; mix well. Spread over baked layer. Sprinkle with mixture of reserved crumbs and nuts. Bake at 350 degrees for 12 minutes or until set. Cool slightly. Cut into squares. Cool completely. Store in refrigerator.

Carla Evens, Wyoming

DATE AND ORANGE SLICE BARS

8 oz. dates, chopped
½ c. sugar
2 tbsp. flour
¾ c. shortening
1 c. packed brown sugar
2 eggs
1 tsp. vanilla extract
1 tsp. soda
1¾ c. flour
½ tsp. salt
½ c. chopped nuts (opt.)
1 15-oz. package candy orange slices

Combine dates, sugar, 2 tablespoons flour and 1 cup water in saucepan. Cook until thick, stirring constantly. Cool. Cream shortening and brown sugar in bowl until light and fluffy. Add eggs; mix well. Add vanilla and soda dissolved in 2 tablespoons hot water.

Stir in 1¾ cups flour, salt and nuts. Cut orange slices lengthwise into thirds. Layer half the batter, orange slices and date mixture in greased 9x13-inch baking pan. Top with remaining batter. Bake at 350 degrees for 35 to 40 minutes. Cool. Cut into bars.

Cindi Sweedler, Iowa

DATE BARS

    1 c. flour
    ¾ c. sugar
    ½ tsp. baking powder
    ¼ tsp. salt
    1 stick margarine, melted
    1 c. chopped dates
    1 c. chopped nuts
    2 eggs, beaten
    1 tsp. vanilla extract

Sift flour, sugar, baking powder and salt into bowl. Stir in melted margarine. Add dates and nuts; mix well. Stir in eggs and vanilla. Pour into greased and floured 9x9-inch baking pan. Bake at 350 degrees for 20 minutes. Cool. Cut into bars.

Margaret Shields, North Carolina

DATE-NUT PINWHEELS

    ¼ c. butter, softened
    ¼ c. shortening
    1 c. packed brown sugar
    1 egg
    ½ tsp. vanilla extract
    1¾ c. flour
    ½ tsp. soda
    ¼ tsp. salt
    12 oz. dates, chopped
    ⅓ c. sugar
    ½ c. finely chopped nuts

Cream butter, shortening, brown sugar, egg and vanilla in bowl until light and fluffy. Add mixture of dry ingredients; mix well. Chill in refrigerator. Cook dates, sugar and ⅓ cup water in saucepan until slightly thickened, stirring constantly. Cool. Stir in nuts. Divide dough into 2 portions. Roll each portion into 7x11-inch rectangle. Spread with date mixture. Roll as for jelly roll from long side; seal edges. Wrap in plastic wrap. Chill for several hours. Cut into ¼-inch slices. Place on lightly greased cookie sheet. Bake at 400 degrees for 10 minutes or until light brown. Cool on wire rack. Yield: 6 dozen.

Marrie Moir, New Mexico

FATTIGMAND

    3 egg yolks
    1 whole egg
    ½ tsp. salt
    ¼ c. confectioners' sugar
    1 tbsp. rum extract
    1 tsp. vanilla extract
    1 c. flour
    Oil for deep frying

Beat egg yolks, egg and salt in mixer bowl for 10 minutes or until very stiff. Blend in confectioners' sugar and flavorings. Add flour; mix well. Knead on lightly floured surface for 7 minutes or until blistered. Roll very thinly; cut into 2x4-inch diamonds. Cut 1-inch slit in center; draw 1 long corner through slit. Deep-fry in 375-degree oil for 30 seconds; turn over. Deep-fry until golden brown. Drain on paper towels. Sprinkle with additional confectioners' sugar. Yield: 3 dozen.

Hulda Pierman, Nebraska

FIG-FILLED COOKIES

    1½ c. chopped figs
    1½ c. sugar
    1 tbsp. butter
    1 c. chopped nuts
    1 tsp. lemon juice
    1 c. shortening
    1 c. packed brown sugar
    3 eggs
    3½ c. flour
    1 tsp. each salt, soda
    1 tbsp. vanilla extract

Combine figs, ½ cup sugar, butter, nuts and lemon juice in double boiler. Cook until thickened, stirring frequently. Cool. Cream shortening, 1 cup sugar and brown sugar in mixer bowl until light and fluffy. Add eggs 1 at a time, beating well after each addition. Add remaining ingredients; mix well. Roll on floured surface. Cut with cookie cutter. Spread half the cookies with fig mixture. Top with remaining cookies; seal edges. Place on ungreased cookie sheet. Bake at 325 degrees for 15 minutes. Cool on wire rack. Yield: 3 dozen.

Laura M Cawley, California

◆◆◆◆◆◆◆◆◆◆◆◆◆◆◆◆◆◆◆◆◆◆◆◆◆◆◆◆◆◆

Hint: *Use 3 small or medium eggs for every 2 large eggs required. If size is unspecified, large eggs should be used.*

◆◆◆◆◆◆◆◆◆◆◆◆◆◆◆◆◆◆◆◆◆◆◆◆◆◆◆◆◆◆

FIG COOKIES

1 c. dried figs
½ c. shortening
¾ c. sugar
2 eggs, well beaten
½ c. honey
2 tbsp. milk
2¾ c. sifted flour
1 tbsp. baking powder
½ tsp. salt
3 tbsp. grated orange rind
1½ c. coconut
1 tsp. lemon extract

Combine figs and water to cover in saucepan. Simmer for 10 minutes. Drain and chop. Cream shortening and sugar in large bowl until light and fluffy. Add eggs 1 at a time, beating well after each addition. Add honey and milk; mix well. Sift flour, baking powder and salt into creamed mixture; mix well. Add figs, orange rind, coconut and lemon flavoring; mix well. Drop by teaspoonfuls onto greased cookie sheet. Bake at 425 degrees for 12 minutes or until light brown. Cool on wire rack. Yield: 3 dozen.

Janeene Shields, Texas

FILBERT SWIRLS

1 c. butter, softened
1 c. sugar
1 egg
1 tsp. vanilla extract
2½ c. flour
½ tsp. baking powder
¼ tsp. nutmeg
¾ c. ground filberts
1 tbsp. confectioners' sugar

Cream butter and sugar in bowl until light and fluffy. Add egg and vanilla; mix well. Sift in flour, baking powder and nutmeg; mix well. Stir in filberts. Spoon into pastry bag fitted with ½-inch plain tip. Pipe into spirals on greased cookie sheet. Bake at 350 degrees for 10 minutes or just until firm and golden brown. Cool on cookie sheet for 5 minutes. Remove to wire rack to cool completely. Sprinkle with confectioners' sugar. Yield: 3 dozen.

Clara Schwintz, Nebraska

FORTUNE COOKIES

3 whites of extra-large eggs
¾ c. sugar
⅛ tsp. salt
½ c. butter, melted
¼ tsp. vanilla extract
1 c. unbleached flour
2 tbsp. strong cold tea
Fortunes written on small paper slips

Beat egg whites until frothy. Beat in sugar and salt. Stir in butter, vanilla, flour and tea 1 at a time. Chill for 30 to 45 minutes. Place 1½ to 2 measuring teaspoonfuls batter on lightly greased cookie sheet; spread with back of spoon into 3-inch circle. Make a second circle leaving at least 4 inches between. **Hint:** *Make only 2 cookies at a time.* Bake at 350 degrees for 5 minutes or until brown around edge and evenly brown on bottom. Remove to wire rack immediately. Place 1 fortune on center of 1 cookie; fold over to enclose fortune. Hold rounded edges together in center with hand, pushing folded edge toward rounded edge with forefinger of other hand and shaping ends of folded edge around forefinger with thumb and middle finger. Place open edge up in muffin cup. Work quickly while cookie is warm and pliable. Repeat with remaining cookie and batter. Cool completely in muffin cups. Store in airtight container. Yield: 2 dozen.
Note: May substitute margarine for butter and bake on greased foil-lined cookie sheet. Cookies will be thinner. Avoid making fortune cookies on humid days.

Frances Gates, California

FRUIT BARS

¼ c. margarine, softened
6 tbsp. brown sugar
¼ c. honey
4¼ c. whole grain wheat flakes
½ c. whole wheat flour
⅔ c. finely chopped mixed dried fruit
1 egg, slightly beaten
½ tsp. cinnamon
¼ tsp. cloves
½ c. chopped nuts

Cream margarine, ¼ cup brown sugar and honey in large bowl until light and fluffy. Crush 4 cups cereal. Add to honey mixture. Stir in ¼ cup flour. Press half the cereal mixture into buttered 8-inch square baking pan. Bake at 350 degrees for 5 minutes. Combine dried fruit with ½ cup boiling water in bowl. Let stand for 5 minutes. Stir in egg, 2 tablespoons brown sugar, ¼ cup cereal, ¼ cup flour, spices and nuts. Spread over baked layer. Sprinkle remaining cereal mixture over top. Bake at 350 degrees for 30 minutes. Cool. Cut into bars.

Angela Turner, Georgia

FRUITCAKE SQUARES

½ c. flour
½ c. Kellogg's All-Bran
1 tsp. baking powder
1 c. coarsely chopped candied pineapple
¾ c. whole candied cherries
¾ c. coarsely chopped dates
½ c. chopped dried apricots
2 eggs
⅓ c. sugar
1½ c. nut halves

Mix first 3 ingredients in bowl. Add fruit; mix well. Beat eggs in mixer bowl until frothy. Beat in sugar gradually. Stir in fruit mixture and nuts. Pour into greased and floured 9-inch square baking pan. Be sure fruits and nuts are evenly distributed. Bake at 300 degrees for 50 minutes or until toothpick inserted near center comes out clean. Cool. Cut into 1½-inch squares. Decorate as desired. Wrap tightly. Store at room temperature for 1 week or longer for improved flavor. Yield: 3 dozen.

Photograph for this recipe on page 6.

GINGERBREAD PEOPLE

½ c. margarine, softened
¾ c. sugar
½ c. molasses
2¼ c. flour
1 c. Planters cocktail peanuts, ground
½ tsp. soda
¾ tsp. ginger
¼ tsp. nutmeg
⅛ tsp. allspice

Cream margarine and sugar in mixer bowl until light and fluffy. Add molasses and ¼ cup water; mix well. Add mixture of flour, ground peanuts, soda, ginger, nutmeg and allspice gradually, beating constantly at low speed. Chill for several hours. Roll to ⅛-inch thickness on well-floured surface. Cut with 5-inch gingerbread cutter; place on greased cookie sheet. Decorate with currants, candied cherries and peanuts for eyes, nose, buttons and other features. Bake at 375 degrees for 8 to 10 minutes. Cool on wire rack. Add additional decoration with confectioners' sugar icing. Yield: 2 dozen.

Photograph for this recipe on this page.

GINGERSNAPS

1 c. shortening
2 c. sugar
2 eggs
1 c. molasses
4 c. flour
1 tsp. cinnamon
2 tsp. ginger
½ tsp. each cloves, salt
1 tbsp. soda

Cream shortening and sugar in bowl until light and fluffy. Add eggs; mix well. Add molasses; mix well. Sift in remaining ingredients; mix well. Shape by tablespoonfuls into balls. Place on greased cookie sheet; flatten slightly. Sprinkle with additional sugar. Bake at 375 degrees for 8 minutes or until light brown. Cool on wire rack. Yield: 5-6 dozen.

Lois Pagnette, Wisconsin

GRANOLA BARS

3½ c. oats
½ c. flaked coconut
⅔ c. melted margarine
½ c. packed brown sugar
⅓ c. honey
1 egg, beaten
½ tsp. vanilla extract
½ tsp. salt

Spread oats in two 10x15-inch baking pans. Bake at 350 degrees for 15 minutes or until light brown. Combine with remaining ingredients in bowl; mix well. Press into greased 10x15-inch baking pan. Bake at 350 degrees for 20 minutes. Cool. Cut into bars.

Jodie Brightman, California

GUMDROP BARS

3 eggs
2 c. packed brown sugar
¼ c. evaporated milk
2 c. cake flour
¼ tsp. salt
1 tsp. cinnamon
1 c. chopped soft gumdrops
½ c. chopped pecans

Beat eggs in bowl. Add brown sugar and evaporated milk gradually; beat well. Add sifted dry ingredients ⅓ at a time, beating well after each addition. Stir in gumdrops and pecans. Spread in greased 9x13-inch baking pan. Bake at 325 degrees for 35 minutes. Cool. Cut into bars. Frost with favorite frosting. Garnish with additional gumdrops.
Note: Omit licorice gumdrops.

Michele Pylant, Tennessee

HIGH FIBER BARS

½ c. milk
½ c. honey
½ c. margarine
½ c. packed brown sugar
1 c. All-Bran
¼ c. wheat germ
1 c. oats
1 c. cornflakes
½ c. sunflower seed
½ c. chopped walnuts
¼ c. sesame seed
½ c. coconut

Combine milk, honey, margarine and brown sugar in large saucepan. Bring to a boil. Cook for 5 minutes. Remove from heat. Add remaining ingredients; mix well. Pat into greased 9x13-inch baking pan. Let stand until firm. Cut into bars.

Cathy Ashby, California

HERMITS

1 c. packed brown sugar
¼ c. shortening
¼ c. margarine, softened
¼ c. cold coffee
1 egg
½ tsp. each soda, salt
½ tsp. each cinnamon, nutmeg
1¾ c. flour
1¼ c. raisins
¾ c. chopped nuts

Cream brown sugar, shortening, margarine, coffee, egg, soda, salt and spices in bowl until light and fluffy. Add flour; mix well. Stir in raisins and nuts. Drop by rounded teaspoonfuls 2 inches apart onto ungreased cookie sheet. Bake at 375 degrees for 8 minutes or until almost firm. Cool on wire rack. Yield: 4 dozen.

Jan Baker, Texas

JELLY BEAN DROPS

½ c. butter, softened
⅓ c. sugar
⅓ c. packed light brown sugar
1 egg
½ tsp. each soda, baking powder and salt
½ tsp. vanilla extract
1¼ c. flour
½ c. oats
1 c. miniature jelly beans

Cream butter and sugars in bowl until light and fluffy. Add egg, soda, baking powder, salt and vanilla; mix well. Add flour and oats; mix well. Stir in jelly beans. Drop by teaspoonfuls onto lightly greased cookie sheet. Bake at 375 degrees for 10 minutes or until light brown. Cool on wire rack. Yield: 3½ dozen.

Troy Gaines, New york

HONEY SNAPS

¾ c. shortening
1 c. packed brown sugar
1 egg
⅓ c. honey
1 tsp. grated lemon rind
2 c. sifted flour
1½ tsp. soda
1 tsp. salt
½ tsp. each cinnamon, ginger
¼ tsp. cloves
1 c. finely chopped walnuts

Cream shortening, brown sugar, egg, honey and lemon rind in bowl until light and fluffy. Sift in flour, soda, salt and spices; mix well. Stir in half the walnuts. Chill for 30 minutes. Shape by teaspoonfuls into small balls. Dip tops in remaining ½ cup walnuts; place 2 inches apart on lightly greased cookie sheet. Bake at 350 degrees for 12 minutes or until edges are very light brown. Cookies will seem soft in center. Cool on cookie sheet for 3 to 4 minutes. Remove to wire rack to cool completely. Yield: 3 dozen.

Janet Phillips, Missouri

Recipes on pages 46, 48. ◆

JAM DIAGONALS

½ c. margarine, softened
¼ c. sugar
1 tsp. vanilla extract
⅛ tsp. salt
1¼ c. flour
¼ c. seedless jam
¾ c. confectioners' sugar
4 tsp. lemon juice

Cream margarine, sugar, vanilla and salt in bowl until light and fluffy. Add flour; mix well. Shape into three 9-inch ropes on floured surface. Place on greased cookie sheet. Make ½-inch groove down length of ropes. Fill with jam. Bake at 350 degrees for 12 minutes or until golden. Cool on cookie sheet. Blend confectioners' sugar and lemon juice in bowl until smooth. Drizzle over cooled cookie rolls. Cut diagonally into 1-inch slices. Yield: 2 dozen.

Karen Drake, Alabama

JAN HAGEL

1 c. butter, softened
½ c. sugar
½ c. packed brown sugar
1 egg, separated
2 c. flour
¼ tsp. salt
½ tsp. cinnamon
½ c. chopped almonds

Cream butter and sugars in bowl until light and fluffy. Stir in egg yolk. Add mixture of dry ingredients; mix well. Press into ungreased 10x15-inch baking pan. Beat egg white with 1 tablespoon water. Brush over dough. Sprinkle almonds over top. Bake at 325 degrees for 15 minutes or until golden. Cut into diamond shapes while warm. Cool.

Joann VandenBrink, Washington

KRUMKAKE

1 c. melted butter
1 c. sugar
4 eggs, separated
1 c. flour
1 c. cornstarch
1 tsp. vanilla extract

Cream butter, sugar and egg yolks in bowl until fluffy. Add flour, cornstarch and vanilla; mix well. Fold in stiffly beaten egg whites. Drop by tablespoonfuls onto hot krumkake griddle. Brown lightly. Shape warm

cookie into cone or drape over side of glass to form basket. Cool. Store in airtight container.
Yield: 2 dozen.
Note: Fill with ice cream or whipped cream

Heath Sand, Oklahoma

LACE COOKIES

½ c. corn syrup
½ c. packed brown sugar
½ c. margarine
1 c. flour
1 c. coconut
1 tsp. vanilla extract

Combine corn syrup, brown sugar and margarine in saucepan. Bring to a boil, stirring constantly. Stir in mixture of flour and coconut gradually. Add vanilla. Drop by teaspoonfuls onto greased cookie sheet. Bake at 350 degrees for 8 minutes or until brown. Cool for 4 minutes. Remove to wire rack or drape over rolling pin or broom handle to cool completely. Yield: 4 dozen.

Sandra Roman, New Hampshire

LEBKUCHEN

¾ c. packed brown sugar
1 egg
1 c. honey, warmed
1 tbsp. lemon juice
3 c. sifted flour
½ tsp. each soda, salt
1 tsp. each nutmeg, allspice
1¼ tsp. each cinnamon, cloves
1½ tsp. grated lemon rind
⅓ c. finely chopped citron
⅓ c. finely chopped nuts
2 c. confectioners' sugar

Beat brown sugar and egg in bowl until light and fluffy. Beat in honey and lemon juice. Sift flour, soda, salt and spices together. Add lemon rind and 1 cup dry mixture to honey mixture; beat until smooth. Stir in remaining dry mixture. Add citron and nuts; mix well. Chill, covered, overnight. Roll dough ½ at a time to ¼-inch thickness on lightly floured surface; cut with 2-inch round cookie cutter. Place 2 inches apart on lightly greased cookie sheet. Bake at 375 degrees for 15 minutes. Remove to wire rack. Cool slightly. Blend confectioners' sugar with 3 tablespoons water. Brush over warm cookies. Cool completely. Store in airtight container in cool dry place for 2 to 3 weeks before serving. Yield: 3 dozen.

Clara Schottweiser, Nebraska

◆ *Recipes on pages 11, 16, 19, 25.*

LEMON BONBON COOKIES

1 c. butter, softened
3 c. (about) confectioners' sugar
¾ c. cornstarch
1¼ c. sifted flour
½ c. ground pecans
Fresh lemon juice
Food coloring

Cream butter and ⅓ cup confectioners' sugar in bowl until light and fluffy. Add cornstarch and flour; blend well. Chill until firm enough to handle. Shape into 1-inch balls; roll in pecans. Place on waxed paper; flatten with glass. Place on ungreased cookie sheet. Bake at 350 degrees for 15 minutes. Cool on wire rack. Blend 2 to 3 cups confectioners' sugar with enough lemon juice to make of spreading consistency. Divide into portions. Tint each portion in pastel bonbon shade. Swirl a dollop of frosting on each cookie. Yield: 4 dozen.

Jean Sheriff, Tennessee

LEMON SQUARES

2¼ c. flour
½ c. confectioners' sugar
1 c. butter, softened
4 eggs, slightly beaten
2 c. sugar
Juice and grated rind of 2 lemons

Mix 2 cups flour and confectioners' sugar in bowl. Cut in butter until crumbly. Press into greased 9x13-inch baking pan. Bake at 350 degrees for 20 minutes. Combine eggs, sugar, ¼ cup flour, lemon juice and rind in bowl; mix well. Pour over baked layer. Sprinkle with additional confectioners' sugar. Bake at 350 degrees for 20 minutes or until set. Cool. Cut into squares.

Delores Brown, West Virginia

LEMON CRACKLE SQUARES

½ tsp. salt
2 tbsp. cornstarch
1 c. sugar
2 eggs, beaten
¾ c. margarine
½ tsp. vanilla extract
½ c. lemon juice
¾ c. cracker crumbs
1 c. packed brown sugar
1 c. flour
½ tsp. soda
1 c. shredded coconut

Combine salt, cornstarch, sugar and 1 cup cold water in saucepan; mix well. Cook over medium heat until thickened, stirring constantly. Pour into double boiler. Cook for 10 minutes, stirring occasionally. Stir a small amount of hot mixture into eggs; stir eggs into hot mixture. Cook for 5 minutes longer; remove from heat. Stir in ¼ cup margarine, vanilla and lemon juice. Cool. Mix cracker crumbs, brown sugar and ½ cup melted margarine in bowl. Add flour, soda and coconut; mix well. Press ¾ of the mixture into buttered 9-inch square baking pan. Pour lemon mixture over top. Sprinkle with remaining crumb mixture. Bake at 350 degrees for 15 minutes or until light brown. Chill in refrigerator. Cut into small squares.

Karen Gaither, Indiana

LEMON WHIPPER SNAPPERS

1 2-layer pkg. lemon cake mix
2 c. whipped topping
1 egg
Confectioners' sugar

Combine cake mix, whipped topping and egg in bowl; mix well. Chill for 15 minutes. Drop by teaspoonfuls into confectioners' sugar; roll to coat. Arrange on greased cookie sheet. Bake at 350 degrees for 10 minutes or until golden. Cool on wire rack. Yield: 4 dozen.

Helena Gallon, Florida

LINZER COOKIES

1½ c. sifted flour
¼ c. sugar
½ tsp. each baking powder, salt
and cinnamon
½ c. packed brown sugar
½ c. butter
1 egg, slightly beaten
⅓ c. ground walnuts
½ c. blackberry jam
1 tbsp. flour
1 egg yolk, slightly beaten

Sift 1½ cups flour, sugar, baking powder, salt and cinnamon into bowl. Stir in brown sugar. Cut in butter until crumbly. Stir in egg and walnuts. Reserve ½ cup. Press remaining mixture into ungreased 9-inch square baking pan. Spread with jam. Mix 1 tablespoon flour into reserved mixture. Roll into 6x9-inch rectangle on floured surface. Cut into strips. Arrange strips in lattice pattern over jam. Brush with egg yolk mixed with 1 teaspoon water. Bake at 375 degrees for 25 minutes. Cool. Cut into squares.

Christine Aufdermaur, California

LIME BUTTER COOKIES

10 tbsp. butter, softened
1 c. sugar
1 egg
Grated rind of 1 lime
3 tbsp. fresh lime juice
2½ c. sifted flour
¼ tsp. soda
½ tsp. salt
2 c. sifted confectioners' sugar
1 egg yolk
½ tsp. vanilla extract
Green food coloring

Cream ½ cup butter and sugar in bowl until light and fluffy. Add egg; beat well. Add half the lime rind and 2 tablespoons lime juice; mix well. Sift in flour, soda and salt; mix well. Shape into 2-inch diameter roll. Wrap in plastic wrap. Chill in refrigerator. Cut into ⅛-inch slices. Arrange on greased cookie sheet. Bake at 400 degrees for 10 minutes or until firm. Cool on wire rack. Cream 2 tablespoons butter, confectioners' sugar, egg yolk, remaining lime rind and vanilla in bowl until light and fluffy. Add enough remaining lime juice and food coloring to make of desired consistency and color. Frost cooled cookies. Yield: 4-5 dozen.

Louanne Heinricks, Ohio

MACADAMIA TEA COOKIES

1 c. butter, softened
½ c. confectioners' sugar
1 tsp. vanilla extract
¼ tsp. salt
2½ c. flour
¾ c. finely chopped macadamia nuts

Cream butter, confectioners' sugar and vanilla in bowl until light and fluffy. Add salt and flour; mix well. Stir in macadamia nuts. Shape into 1-inch balls; place on ungreased cookie sheet. Bake at 400 degrees for 10 minutes or until golden brown. Roll warm cookies in additional confectioners' sugar. Cool on wire rack. Yield: 3½ dozen.

Janice K. Ballard, Michigan

MACADAMIA BARS

⅓ c. butter, softened
1 c. flour
⅓ c. packed brown sugar
½ c. chopped macadamia nuts
1 egg
1 8-oz. package cream cheese, softened
¼ c. sugar

2 tbsp. milk
2 tbsp. lemon juice
½ tsp. vanilla extract

Combine butter, flour and brown sugar in bowl. Add nuts. Reserve 1 cup mixture. Pat remaining mixture into ungreased 8-inch square baking dish. Bake at 350 degrees for 12 minutes or until light brown. Combine egg, cream cheese, sugar, milk, lemon juice and vanilla in bowl; beat until smooth. Spread over baked layer. Sprinkle reserved crumb mixture over top. Bake at 350 degrees for 25 minutes or until set. Cool. Cut into bars.

Carol Hall, California

ALMOND MACAROONS

1¼ c. slivered blanched almonds
¾ c. sugar
3 egg whites

Process almonds in blender until finely chopped. Do not chop almonds by hand. Combine almonds, sugar and egg whites in saucepan. Cook over medium heat for 8 to 10 minutes or until very thick and stiff, stirring constantly. Cooked mixture should be consistency of mashed potatoes. Drop by level tablespoonfuls onto greased and floured cookie sheet. Cool to room temperature. Bake in preheated 300-degree oven for 20 minutes or until light golden brown. Remove from cookie sheet immediately to wire rack to cool completely. Yield: 2 dozen.

LaVita Brennan, Minnesota

◆◆◆◆◆◆◆◆◆◆◆◆◆◆◆◆◆◆◆◆◆◆◆◆◆◆◆

Hint: *To store baked cookies, place on edge in empty food wrap boxes. Wrap tightly, label, and store in freezer.*

◆◆◆◆◆◆◆◆◆◆◆◆◆◆◆◆◆◆◆◆◆◆◆◆◆◆◆

EASY CHOCOLATE MACAROONS

1 can sweetened condensed milk
3 sq. unsweetened chocolate
¼ tsp. salt
2 4-oz. cans shredded coconut
1 tsp. vanilla extract

Combine first 3 ingredients in double boiler. Cook until chocolate melts and mixture thickens, stirring frequently; remove from heat. Add coconut and vanilla; mix well. Drop by rounded tablespoonfuls 1 inch apart onto greased cookie sheet. Bake at 350 degrees for 10 minutes or just until set. Cool on wire rack. Yield: 2 dozen.

Beverly Barnes, North Carolina

MACAROON COOKIES

1 stick margarine, softened
1 c. sugar
1 egg
1 c. buttermilk baking mix
1½ c. instant potato flakes
2 tsp. coconut flavoring

Cream margarine and sugar in bowl until light and fluffy. Add egg; mix well. Add remaining ingredients; mix well. Drop by teaspoonfuls onto foil-lined cookie sheet. Bake at 325 degrees for 10 minutes. Yield: 3 dozen.

Ila Bravo, California

OVERNIGHT MACAROONS

4 c. oats
2 c. packed brown sugar
1 c. oil
2 eggs, beaten
1 tsp. salt
1 tsp. almond extract

Mix oats, brown sugar and oil in bowl. Let stand overnight. Add eggs, salt and almond extract; mix well. Drop by teaspoonfuls onto ungreased cookie sheet. Bake at 325 degrees for 15 minutes. Remove to wire rack immediately to cool. Yield: 6 dozen.

Carolyn K. Stephens, Ohio

PECAN MACAROONS

4 egg whites
1 c. sugar
1 tsp. vanilla extract
2 c. pecans

Beat egg whites until soft peaks form. Add ¾ cup sugar gradually, beating until stiff peaks form. Add remaining sugar 1 tablespoon at a time, beating well after each addition. Fold in vanilla and pecans. Drop by spoonfuls onto waxed paper-lined cookie sheet. Bake at 225 degrees for 30 minutes. Cool on wire rack. Yield: 2-3 dozen.

Ann Van Winkle, Texas

RASPBERRY MACAROONS

3 egg whites
⅛ tsp. salt
3½ tbsp. dry raspberry gelatin
¾ c. sugar
1 c. miniature chocolate chips

Beat egg whites with salt until foamy. Add mixture of gelatin and sugar gradually, beating until stiff peaks form. Fold in chocolate chips. Drop by teaspoonfuls onto cookie sheet lined with baking parchment. Bake at 250 degrees for 25 minutes. Turn oven off. Let stand in closed oven for 30 minutes. Cool on wire rack. Yield: 2½ dozen.

Marie Woodyard, Missouri

MALT DROPS

2 c. flour
1 pkg. coconut-pecan frosting mix
1 c. crushed malted milk balls
1 c. butter, softened
½ tsp. soda
2 eggs, beaten

Combine first 5 ingredients in bowl; mix well. Add eggs; mix well. Drop by teaspoonfuls onto greased cookie sheet. Bake at 375 degrees for 8 minutes or until golden brown. Cool on wire rack. Yield: 4-5 dozen.

Barbara Roader, California

MARZIPAN COOKIES

½ c. sugar
¾ c. ground almonds
Grated rind of 1 orange
2 egg yolks
⅛ tsp. almond extract
¼ c. confectioners' sugar
¼ c. sliced almonds

Mix sugar, ground almonds and orange rind in bowl. Add egg yolks and almond flavoring; mix well. Chill for several minutes. Roll ⅛ inch thick on surface sprinkled with confectioners' sugar. Cut with 2-inch cookie cutter. Press several sliced almonds into each cookie. Place on greased cookie sheet. Bake at 375 degrees for 8 minutes or until golden. Cool on wire rack. Yield: 1½ dozen.

Sally Birnbaum, New York

MAPLE SYRUP COOKIES

¾ c. shortening
½ c. packed brown sugar
1 egg
½ c. maple syrup
1 tsp. maple flavoring
2¼ c. flour
2 tsp. baking powder

½ tsp. each soda, salt
½ c. chopped walnuts
3½ dozen walnut halves (opt.)

Cream shortening, brown sugar and egg in bowl until light and fluffy. Add maple syrup and flavoring; mix well. Stir in mixture of dry ingredients. Add chopped walnuts; mix well. Drop by rounded teaspoonfuls onto ungreased cookie sheet. Press walnut half into each cookie. Bake at 400 degrees for 8 minutes or until light brown. Cool on wire rack. Yield: 3½ dozen.

Gloria Garrett, Connecticut

MAYONNAISE COOKIES

1 c. mayonnaise
1 c. sugar
1 tsp. vanilla extract
2 c. flour
1 tsp. soda
½ tsp. salt
1 c. chopped pecans

Mix mayonnaise, sugar and vanilla in bowl. Add remaining ingredients; mix well. Shape into 1-inch balls. Place 3 inches apart on ungreased cookie sheet. Flatten with glass dipped in sugar. Bake at 350 degrees for 10 minutes. Cool on wire rack. Yield: 4 dozen.

Amanda Hunt, California

MEXICAN WEDDING COOKIES

1 c. confectioners' sugar
1 stick butter, softened
1 tsp. vanilla extract
1 c. flour
1 c. finely chopped pecans

Combine confectioners' sugar, butter, vanilla, flour and pecans in bowl; mix well. Shape into balls. Place on ungreased cookie sheet. Bake at 375 degrees for 25 minutes or until light brown. Roll hot cookies in additional confectioners' sugar. Yield: 2 dozen.

Tamara Biermann, California

M AND M COOKIES

1 c. butter, softened
¾ c. sugar
¾ c. packed brown sugar
2 eggs
1 tsp. vanilla extract
2½ c. flour

½ tsp. soda
½ tsp. salt
1 16-oz. package M and M's
1 c. pecans (opt.)

Cream first 3 ingredients in bowl until light and fluffy. Add eggs and vanilla; mix well. Stir in mixture of flour, soda and salt. Add M and M's and pecans; mix well. Drop by spoonfuls onto greased cookie sheet. Bake at 350 degrees for 10 minutes or until brown. Cool on wire rack. Yield: 8 dozen.

Kelly Deas, Texas

MINCEMEAT COOKIES

½ c. shortening
½ c. butter, softened
1 c. sugar
½ c. packed brown sugar
1 tsp. vanilla extract
3 eggs
3¾ c. flour
½ tsp. salt
1 tsp. each soda, cinnamon
1½ c. mincemeat

Cream shortening, butter and sugars in bowl until light and fluffy. Beat in vanilla and eggs. Add mixture of dry ingredients; mix well. Stir in mincemeat. Drop by spoonfuls onto greased cookie sheet. Bake at 350 degrees for 10 minutes. Cool on wire rack. Yield: 5 dozen.

Mrs. Billy Hart, West Virginia

MINCEMEAT PILLOWS

¼ c. shortening
¼ c. butter, softened
¼ c. sugar
¼ c. packed brown sugar
1 egg
1 c. plus 6 tbsp. flour
¼ tsp. soda
½ tsp. salt
¼ c. mincemeat
2 tbsp. finely chopped nuts
1 tbsp. chopped maraschino cherries

Cream first 5 ingredients in bowl until light and fluffy. Add mixture of flour, soda and salt; mix well. Shape into 1½-inch diameter roll. Wrap in plastic wrap. Chill for several hours. Cut into ⅛-inch slices. Place half the cookies on ungreased cookie sheet. Combine remaining ingredients. Place ½ teaspoonful on half the cookies. Top with remaining cookies; seal edges. Bake at 400 degrees for 8 minutes or until light brown. Cool on wire rack. Yield: 2½ dozen.

Amanda Berg, New Jersey

BASIC BROWNIE MIX

6 c. flour
4 tsp. baking powder
4 tsp. salt
8 c. sugar
1 8-oz. can cocoa
2 c. shortening

Sift flour, baking powder and salt into bowl. Stir in sugar and cocoa. Cut in shortening until crumbly. Store in airtight container in cool place for up to 12 weeks. Yield: 16 cups.

Easy Brownies — Combine 4 cups Brownie Mix, 4 beaten eggs and 2 teaspoons vanilla in bowl; mix well. Stir in ½ cup chopped nuts. Spread in greased and floured 10x15-inch baking pan. Bake at 350 degrees for 30 minutes or until brownies pull from edges of pan. Cool. Cut into squares.

Cynthia Harper, Georgia

BASIC COOKIE MIX BAZAAR

4 c. flour
2 c. sugar
2 tsp. baking powder
1½ tsp. salt
1⅓ c. shortening

Mix dry ingredients in bowl. Cut in shortening until crumbly. Store in airtight container at room temperature for up to 6 weeks or freeze for longer storage. Yield: 8½ cups.

Mincemeat-Oatmeal Bars — Combine 2 cups Basic Cookie Mix, ¾ cup oats, 1 egg and 1 tablespoon water in bowl; mix until crumbly. Pat half the mixture into greased 9-inch square baking pan. Add layers of 1 cup mincemeat and remaining oats mixture. Bake at 350 degrees for 30 minutes. Drizzle with ginger-flavored confectioners' sugar glaze. Cool. Cut into bars.
Orange-Coconut Drops — Combine 2½ cups Basic Cookie Mix, ¼ cup orange marmalade, 1 egg, 3 tablespoons orange juice and 1 cup coconut in bowl; mix well. Drop by teaspoonfuls onto greased cookie sheet. Bake at 375 degrees for 8 minutes or until golden brown. Cool on wire rack. Frost with orange butter frosting if desired.
Double Chocolate Drops — Combine 2¼ cups Basic Cookie Mix, 1 egg, ¼ cup milk, 2 ounces melted chocolate, ½ cup chocolate chips and ½ cup chopped nuts in bowl; mix well. Drop by teaspoonfuls onto greased cookie sheet. Bake at 375 degrees for 10 minutes or until set. Cool on wire rack. Frost with chocolate or vanilla frosting if desired. Yield: 2½ dozen.

Caroline White, Colorado

OATMEAL COOKIE MIX

2 c. sugar
2 c. packed brown sugar
3 c. sifted flour
2 tsp. each soda, salt
1 tsp. baking powder
¼ tsp. cinnamon (opt.)
2 c. shortening
6 c. oats

Sift sugar, brown sugar, flour, soda, salt, baking powder and cinnamon into bowl. Cut in shortening until crumbly. Add oats. Store in airtight container in cool place. Yield: 16 cups.

Oatmeal Cookie Mix Cookies — Combine 2 cups Oatmeal Cookie Mix with 1 egg, 1 teaspoon vanilla and ½ cup chopped nuts, raisins, coconut or chocolate chips; mix well. Drop by teaspoonfuls onto greased cookie sheet. Bake at 350 degrees for 12 minutes or until brown. Cool on wire rack. Yield: 2 dozen.
Oatmeal Sandwich Cookies — Fill baked cookies with orange confectioners' sugar icing, peanut butter and honey or melted milk chocolate. Yield: 1 dozen.

Edna Ehle, Ohio

MOCHA PINWHEELS

½ c. butter, softened
¾ c. sugar
1 egg
1 tsp. vanilla extract
1¾ c. flour
½ tsp. baking powder
¼ tsp. salt
1 tsp. instant coffee powder
⅓ c. chopped pecans
1 1-oz. envelope premelted unsweetened chocolate

Cream butter and sugar in bowl until light and fluffy. Add egg and vanilla; mix well. Blend in mixture of flour, baking powder and salt. Divide into 2 portions. Add coffee powder and pecans to 1 portion; mix well. Add chocolate to remaining dough; mix well. Chill both mixtures in refrigerator. Roll each portion into 8x16-inch on rectangle on waxed paper. Place coffee-flavored dough on top fo chocolate-flavored dough. Roll as for jelly roll from long side. Chill, wrapped in waxed paper for 2 hours. Cut into ¼-inch slices. Place on ungreased cookie sheet. Bake at 350 degrees for 9 minutes or until firm. Cool on wire rack. Yield: 5 dozen.

Myrna Hartwig, Nebraska

MORAVIAN COOKIES

½ c. butter
1 c. molasses
⅓ c. packed brown sugar
¾ tsp. each ginger, cloves and cinnamon
¼ tsp. each nutmeg, allspice
Dash of salt
¾ tsp. soda
3¾ c. sifted flour

Combine butter and molasses in saucepan. Heat until butter is melted; remove from heat. Stir in remaining ingredients except flour. Add flour gradually; mix well. Wrap tightly in plastic wrap. Chill for 1 week. Roll thinly on lightly floured surface. Cut with cookie cutter. Place on greased cookie sheet. Punch hole for hangers if desired. Bake at 350 degrees until golden brown. Cool on wire rack. Decorate as desired. Yield: 5 dozen.

Willa Warden, North Carolina

◆◆◆◆◆◆◆◆◆◆◆◆◆◆◆◆◆◆◆◆◆◆◆◆◆◆◆◆◆◆◆

Hint: *For easier cutting, dip cookie cutter into flour.*

◆◆◆◆◆◆◆◆◆◆◆◆◆◆◆◆◆◆◆◆◆◆◆◆◆◆◆◆◆◆◆

OLD-FASHIONED MOLASSES COOKIES

1 c. molasses
1 c. melted shortening
1 c. sugar
3½ tsp. soda
1 c. buttermilk
5¼ c. flour
1 tsp. each ginger, salt
½ tsp. cinnamon

Combine molasses, shortening and sugar in bowl; mix well. Dissolve soda in buttermilk. Stir into molasses mixture. Add sifted dry ingredients; mix well. Roll ¼ inch thick on floured surface. Cut with cookie cutter. Place on greased cookie sheet. Bake at 400 degrees for 12 minutes. Cool on wire rack. Yield: 5 dozen.

Joan Russell, Maine

MOLASSES CRACKER JILLS

½ c. butter, softened
1 3-oz. package cream cheese, softened
1¼ c. packed brown sugar
1 egg
2 c. flour
¼ c. molasses
¼ tsp. soda
1 c. salted Spanish peanuts
2 c. coarsely crushed soda crackers
½ c. sugar

Cream butter, cream cheese and brown sugar in bowl until light and fluffy. Add egg; mix well. Add flour alternately with mixture of molasses and soda, mixing well after each addition. Fold in peanuts and crackers. Chill, covered, for 2 hours. Shape by teaspoonfuls into balls. Roll in sugar. Place on ungreased cookie sheet. Bake at 375 degrees for 10 minutes or until light brown. Cool on wire rack. Yield: 4½-5 dozen.

Darlene Koenig, South Dakota

NECTARINE COOKIES

2 c. flour
1 tsp. each soda, salt
¼ tsp. cinnamon
⅛ tsp. cloves
½ c. butter, softened
1⅓ c. sugar
1 egg
½ c. chopped roasted almonds
½ c. raisins
1½ c. chopped nectarines

Sift flour, soda, salt and spices together. Cream butter and sugar in bowl until light and fluffy. Add egg; mix well. Stir in almonds and raisins. Add sifted ingredients alternately with nectarines, mixing well after each addition. Drop by tablespoonfuls onto greased cookie sheet. Bake at 375 degrees for 15 minutes or until light brown. Cool on wire rack. Store in loosely covered container. Yield: 3-4 dozen.

Jewell Montgomery, Texas

NUTMEG COOKIES

¼ c. butter, softened
1½ c. sugar
2 eggs
2½ c. flour
¼ tsp. salt
1 tsp. each soda, nutmeg
1 c. sour cream

Cream butter and sugar in bowl until light and fluffy. Add eggs; mix well. Sift in flour, salt, soda and nutmeg. Stir in sour cream. Drop by tablespoonfuls onto greased cookie sheet. Bake at 375 degrees for 12 minutes or just until firm and golden brown. Cool on wire rack. Yield: 3 dozen.

Cindy Bell, Virginia

SAUCY OAT COOKIES

1¾ c. quick-cooking oats
1½ c. flour
1 tsp. each salt, baking powder, cinnamon
½ tsp. each nutmeg, soda
½ c. butter, softened
1 c. packed brown sugar
½ c. sugar
1 egg, slightly beaten
¾ c. applesauce
1 c. chocolate chips
1 c. raisins
1 c. chopped nuts

Combine first 7 dry ingredients in bowl; mix well. Cream butter and sugars in bowl until light and fluffy. Add egg; mix well. Add oats mixture alternately with applesauce, mixing well after each addition. Stir in chocolate chips, raisins and nuts. Drop by level tablespoonfuls onto greased cookie sheet. Bake at 375 degrees for 15 minutes. Cool on wire rack. Yield: 8 dozen.

Susan Laffredo, Pennsylvania

OATMEAL-BANANA COOKIES

1½ c. flour
1 c. sugar
1 tsp. salt
½ tsp. soda
¼ tsp. nutmeg
¾ tsp. cinnamon
1¼ c. oil
1 egg
3 lg. bananas, mashed
½ c. chopped walnuts
1¾ c. oats

Combine flour, sugar, salt, soda and spices in bowl. Add oil and egg; mix well. Add bananas; mix well. Stir in walnuts and oats. Drop by spoonfuls onto ungreased cookie sheet. Bake at 350 degrees until golden brown. Cool on wire rack. Yield: 5 dozen.

Helen Windham, Florida

WORLD'S BEST OATMEAL COOKIES

1¼ c. oats
1 c. sifted flour
½ c. sugar
½ c. packed brown sugar
1 c. coconut
½ c. chocolate chips
½ tsp. each salt, soda

½ c. oil
1 egg, beaten
1 tsp. vanilla extract

Combine dry ingredients in bowl; mix well. Add oil, egg and vanilla; mix well. Mixture will be dry. Shape into 1-inch balls. Place on ungreased cookie sheet. Bake at 325 degrees for 12 to 15 minutes. Cool on wire rack. Yield: 3½ dozen.

Mary George, Tennessee

OATMEAL KISS COOKIES

¼ c. butter, softened
¼ c. shortening
½ c. sugar
½ c. packed light brown sugar
1 egg
1 c. flour
½ tsp. each soda, salt
1 c. quick-cooking oats
½ c. chopped nuts
36 milk chocolate kisses

Cream butter, shortening and sugars in bowl until light and fluffy. Add egg; mix well. Add mixture of flour, soda and salt; mix well. Stir in oats and nuts. Shape into 1-inch balls. Place on ungreased cookie sheet. Bake at 375 degrees for 10 minutes or until light brown. Remove from oven. Place chocolate kiss in center of each cookie; press lightly. Cool on wire rack. Yield: 3 dozen.

Photograph for this recipe on page 1.

WHOLE WHEAT OATMEAL COOKIES

1 stick margarine, softened
½ c. sugar
¼ c. packed brown sugar
1 egg
½ tsp. cinnamon
¼ tsp. nutmeg
1¼ c. oats
1 c. whole wheat flour
½ tsp. each salt, soda
½ c. raisins (opt.)
½ c. chopped nuts (opt.)

Cream margarine and sugars in bowl until light and fluffy. Add egg; mix well. Stir in mixture of dry ingredients. Add raisins and nuts; mix well. Drop by rounded teaspoonfuls onto greased cookie sheet. Bake at 350 degrees for 10 minutes or until brown. Cool on wire rack. Yield: 3½ dozen.

Carmelita P. Antosek, North Carolina

OATMEAL SCOTCHIES

1 c. butter, softened
3/4 c. sugar
3/4 c. packed brown sugar
2 eggs
1 tsp. vanilla extract
1 c. flour
1 tsp. soda
1/2 tsp. each salt, cinnamon
3 c. oats
1   12-oz. package butterscotch chips

Cream butter, sugars, eggs and vanilla in bowl until light and fluffy. Add combined flour, soda and spices gradually. Stir in oats and butterscotch chips. Drop by spoonfuls onto ungreased cookie sheet. Bake at 375 degrees for 7 minutes or until light brown. Yield: 4 dozen.

Nancy Voogd, California

OATMEAL-CHOCOLATE CHIP COOKIES

1 stick margarine, softened
1/2 c. shortening
3 eggs
1 c. packed brown sugar
1 c. sugar
1 tsp. each soda, salt
2 tsp. vanilla extract
2 c. oats
2 1/4 c. flour
1 c. chocolate chips
1 c. chopped nuts (opt.)

Cream margarine, shortening, eggs and sugars in large mixer bowl for 5 minutes. Stir in soda, salt and vanilla. Add oats; mix well. Add flour; stir just until moistened. Stir in chocolate chips and nuts. Drop by teaspoonfuls onto greased cookie sheet. Bake at 350 degrees for 10 minutes. Cool for 1 minute before removing from cookie sheet. Cool on wire rack. Yield: 8 dozen.

Helen Hauser, South Carolina

OATMEAL-RAISIN COOKIES

2 c. flour
2 c. oats
1 c. sugar
1 tsp. cinnamon
1/8 tsp. salt
1 c. shortening
3 eggs
1 tsp. vanilla extract
1 tsp. soda
1/4 c. milk
1 c. raisins
1 c. chopped nuts

Combine first 5 dry ingredients in bowl. Cut in shortening until crumbly. Add eggs and vanilla; mix well. Stir in mixture of soda and milk. Fold in raisins and nuts; mix well. Drop by teaspoonfuls onto greased cookie sheet. Bake at 350 degrees for 10 minutes or until golden brown. Cool on wire rack. Yield: 5 dozen.

Teresa Schultz, Kentucky

ORANGE PINWHEELS

3/4 c. butter, softened
1 c. sugar
1 egg
1 1/2 tsp. grated orange rind
3 tbsp. orange juice
2 c. flour
1 tsp. baking powder
1/2 tsp. salt
1   6-oz. package semisweet chocolate chips
2 tbsp. butter
1 c. finely chopped nuts

Cream 3/4 cup butter and sugar in bowl until light and fluffy. Add egg, orange rind and 1 tablespoon orange juice; mix well. Stir in mixture of flour, baking powder and salt. Reserve 2/3 cup dough. Chill remaining dough, covered, for 1 hour. Melt chocolate chips with 2 tablespoons butter in saucepan over low heat; remove from heat. Stir in nuts, 2 tablespoons orange juice and reserved 2/3 cup dough. Roll chilled dough into 12x16-inch rectangle on floured surface. Spread with chocolate mixture. Roll as for jelly roll from long side; seal edges. Chill, wrapped in plastic wrap, in refrigerator. Cut into 1/4-inch slices. Place on ungreased cookie sheet. Bake at 350 degrees for 10 minutes or until light brown. Cool on wire rack. Yield: 5 dozen.

Janet Latham, Idaho

◆◆◆◆◆◆◆◆◆◆◆◆◆◆◆◆◆◆◆◆◆◆◆◆◆

Hint: *To vary refrigerator cookies, roll unsliced logs in chopped nuts, coconut or grated chocolate. Slice and bake as directed.*

◆◆◆◆◆◆◆◆◆◆◆◆◆◆◆◆◆◆◆◆◆◆◆◆◆

ORANGE-PECAN KISS COOKIES

½ c. butter, softened
½ c. sugar
1 egg
1 tsp. vanilla extract
1 tsp. grated orange rind
1¼ c. flour
¼ tsp. soda
⅛ tsp. salt
½ c. finely chopped pecans
30 milk chocolate kisses

Cream butter, sugar, egg, vanilla and orange rind in bowl until light and fluffy. Add mixture of flour, soda and salt; beat well. Chill until dough is easily handled. Shape into 1-inch balls. Roll in chopped pecans. Place on ungreased cookie sheet. Bake at 350 degrees for 10 minutes. Remove from oven. Place chocolate kiss in center of each cookie; press lightly. Cool on wire rack. Yield: 2½ dozen.

Photograph for this recipe on page 1.

SWEETHEART COOKIES

3½ c. flour
¾ c. sugar
2½ tsp. grated orange rind
¼ tsp. salt
1½ c. butter
5 to 6 tbsp. Florida orange juice
1½ c. confectioners' sugar

Combine flour, sugar, 2 teaspoons orange rind and salt in bowl. Cut in 1¼ cups butter until crumbly. Add ¼ cup orange juice; mix just until mixture holds together. Press into ball. Chill, covered, for 30 minutes. Roll ⅛ inch thick on lightly floured surface. Cut with 2-inch cookie cutter. Cut holes in centers of half the cookies if desired. Place on ungreased cookie sheet. Bake at 400 degrees for 8 minutes. Cool on wire rack. Cream ¼ cup butter, confectioners' sugar, 1 to 2 tablespoons orange juice and ½ teaspoon orange rind in bowl until light and fluffy. Spread on solid cookies. Top with cut-out cookies.
Yield: 6 dozen.

Photograph for this recipe on page 87.

PEANUT BUTTER-OAT BARS

2 c. quick-cooking oats
⅔ c. Skippy super chunk peanut butter
2 tbsp. Mazola margarine
1 c. sugar
⅓ c. Karo dark corn syrup
2 eggs

1 tsp. vanilla extract
1½ c. flour
1 tsp. baking powder
¼ tsp. salt
2 c. raisins

Spread oats in 10x15-inch baking pan. Bake at 400 degrees for 8 minutes or until lightly toasted, stirring occasionally. Cool. Cream peanut butter and margarine in bowl until light and fluffy. Add sugar, corn syrup, eggs and vanilla; beat well. Add mixture of flour, baking powder and salt; beat well. Stir in oats and raisins. Spread in greased 9x13-inch baking dish. Bake at 350 degrees for 25 minutes. Cool on wire rack. Cut into 1x3-inch bars. Store individually wrapped or in airtight container.

Photograph for this recipe on page 35.

OLD-FASHIONED PEANUT BUTTER COOKIES

1 c. shortening
1 c. peanut butter
1 c. packed brown sugar
1 c. sugar
2 eggs, beaten
2½ c. flour, sifted
1 tsp. each soda, baking powder
¼ tsp. salt

Cream shortening and peanut butter in bowl. Add sugars gradually; mix well. Stir in eggs. Add sifted dry ingredients; mix well. Chill in refrigerator. Shape into balls. Place on greased cookie sheet. Flatten with fork dipped in flour. Bake at 350 degrees for 15 minutes or until light brown. Cool on wire rack.
Yield: 6 dozen.

Sharon Williams, North Carolina

PEACH DROPS

½ c. margarine, softened
1   3-oz. package cream cheese, softened
¼ c. packed brown sugar
¾ c. peach preserves
1¼ c. flour
1½ tsp. baking powder
1 tsp. cinnamon
¼ tsp. salt
½ c. walnuts
1 c. confectioners' sugar
1 tbsp. margarine, melted

Cream ½ cup margarine, cream cheese and brown sugar in bowl until light and fluffy. Add ½ cup preserves; mix well. Add mixture of next 4 ingredients;

mix well. Stir in walnuts. Drop by spoonfuls onto greased cookie sheet. Bake at 350 degrees for 12 minutes. Cool on wire rack. Blend confectioners' sugar, melted margarine and ¼ cup preserves in bowl. Frost cooled cookies. Yield: 3 dozen.

Nelda Love, Oklahoma

THREE-WAY PEANUT BUTTER COOKIES

½ c. butter, softened
⅓ c. peanut butter
½ c. sugar
¼ c. packed brown sugar
1 egg
2 tbsp. milk
1 tsp. vanilla extract
2¼ c. flour
¼ tsp. each baking powder, salt
2 oz. unsweetened chocolate, melted
Semisweet chocolate, melted (opt.)
Salted peanuts, chopped (opt.)

Cream butter and peanut butter in bowl. Add sugars gradually, creaming until light and fluffy. Beat in egg, milk and vanilla. Add mixture of flour, baking powder and salt; mix well. Divide into 2 portions, 1 slightly larger than the other. Add chocolate to smaller portion; mix well. Shape as desired. Bake all cookies at 350 degrees for 10 to 14 minutes or until firm.

Layer Bars — Divide each dough into 2 portions. Roll each portion into 8-inch square between waxed paper. Stack alternate layers of chocolate and peanut butter dough on tray. Chill, covered, for several hours to overnight. Cut into bars; place on ungreased cookie sheet. Bake as above. Garnish with drizzle of melted semisweet chocolate.
Two-Tone Cookies — Roll peanut butter dough into 6x14-inch rectangle between waxed paper. Shape chocolate dough into 14-inch log. Place on rectangle; roll to enclose log. Chill, covered, for several hours to overnight. Cut into ¼-inch slices; place on ungreased cookie sheet. Press chopped peanuts on top. Bake as above. Cool on wire rack.
Pinwheel Lollipops — Roll each dough into 8x14-inch rectangle between waxed paper. Place chocolate dough on peanut butter dough; roll as for jelly roll from long side. Chill, covered, for several hours to overnight. Slice ¼ inch thick. Arrange 5-inch wooden skewers on ungreased cookie sheet. Press cookie slice on each stick to form lollipop. Bake as above. Cool on wire rack.

Photograph for this recipe on this page.

PEANUT BUTTER KISS BARS

½ c. creamy peanut butter
¼ c. butter
1 c. packed light brown sugar
2 eggs
1 tsp. vanilla extract
⅔ c. flour
1 c. chopped peanuts
16 milk chocolate kisses

Cream first 3 ingredients in bowl until light and fluffy. Add eggs and vanilla; beat well. Stir in flour and ¾ cup peanuts. Spread in 9-inch square baking pan. Sprinkle remaining ¼ cup peanuts on top. Bake at 350 degrees for 25 minutes. Remove from oven. Press kisses evenly over baked layer. Cool completely. Cut into bars with chocolate kiss in center of each.

Photograph for this recipe on page 1.

EASY PEANUT BUTTER COOKIES

1 c. peanut butter
1 c. sugar
1 egg
1 tsp. vanilla extract (opt.)

Combine all ingredients in bowl; mix well. Shape into 1½-inch balls. Place on greased cookie sheet. Flatten with glass dipped in additional sugar. Bake at 350 degrees for 10 minutes. Cool on cookie sheet until firm. Remove to wire rack to cool completely. Yield: 1 dozen.

Lisa Shankle, North Carolina

PEANUT BRITTLE CRISPS

1/4 c. butter, softened
1/4 c. shortening
1/4 c. sugar
1 egg
1 1/4 c. flour
1/2 tsp. soda
1/4 tsp. salt
1 c. finely crushed peanut brittle

Cream butter, shortening and sugar in bowl until light and fluffy. Add egg; mix well. Stir in dry ingredients. Fold in peanut brittle. Shape by teaspoonfuls into balls. Place on ungreased cookie sheet. Bake at 375 degrees for 8 minutes. Cool for 1 minute. Remove to wire rack to cool completely. Yield: 3 dozen.

Pam Longmire, Oklahoma

WHOLE WHEAT ORANGE-PEANUT BUTTER COOKIES

1/2 c. Mazola margarine, softened
1/2 c. Skippy super chunk peanut butter
2/3 c. packed light brown sugar
1/3 c. sugar
1 egg
2 tsp. grated orange rind
1/2 tsp. vanilla extract
1 1/4 c. whole wheat flour
1/2 tsp. each baking powder, soda
1/8 tsp. salt

Cream margarine, peanut butter and sugars in bowl until light and fluffy. Add egg, orange rind and vanilla; beat well. Add mixture of dry ingredients; beat well. Chill, covered, for 1 hour. Shape into 1-inch balls. Roll in additional sugar. Place 2 inches apart on ungreased cookie sheet. Flatten with lightly sugared fork, making crisscross design. Bake at 350 degrees for 12 minutes or until light brown. Cool on wire rack. Store in airtight container. Yield: 3 dozen.

Photograph for this recipe on page 35.

GOLDEN PEAR DROPS

1/2 c. butter, softened
3/4 c. packed brown sugar
1 egg
1/2 c. sour cream
1 3/4 c. flour
1 tsp. soda
1/2 tsp. salt
1/2 tsp. peppermint extract
1 c. chopped canned pears, drained
1 c. chopped black walnuts
1/4 c. chopped maraschino cherries, drained
60 maraschino cherry halves

Cream butter and brown sugar in bowl until light and fluffy. Add egg and sour cream; mix well. Stir in dry ingredients and flavoring. Add pears, walnuts and chopped cherries; mix well. Drop by teaspoonfuls onto lightly greased cookie sheet. Top each with maraschino cherry half. Bake at 375 degrees for 15 to 18 minutes. Cool for 1 minute. Remove to wire rack to cool completely. Yield: 5 dozen.

Tamara Kent, Missouri

MICROWAVE PECAN BARS

1/2 c. butter, melted
1 16-oz. package light brown sugar
2 eggs, beaten
2 tsp. vanilla extract
2 c. chopped pecans
1 1/2 c. pancake mix
2 c. confectioners' sugar

Combine first 4 ingredients in bowl; mix well. Add pecans and pancake mix; mix well. Pour into greased 8x12-inch glass baking dish. Microwave on High for 8 to 10 minutes, turning dish every 3 minutes. Center will appear soft. Cool completely. Cut into bars. Roll in confectioners' sugar to coat.

Bonnie Stover, Florida

PEANUT WHIRLIGIGS

1/2 c. butter, softened
1/2 c. shortening
1 3-oz. package cream cheese, softened
1 c. sugar
1 tsp. vanilla extract
2 c. flour
1/2 tsp. salt
3/4 c. finely chopped salted peanuts
1/4 c. melted butter
1 6-oz. package semisweet chocolate chips, melted

Cream softened butter, shortening, cream cheese and sugar in bowl until light and fluffy. Add vanilla; mix well. Stir in flour and salt. Add peanuts; mix well. Chill in refrigerator. Divide into 2 portions. Roll each portion into 9x16-inch rectangle on floured surface. Spread with mixture of melted butter and chocolate. Roll as for jelly roll from short side. Wrap in plastic wrap. Chill for 2 hours or longer. Cut into 1/8-inch slices. Place on ungreased cookie sheet. Bake at 375 degrees for 7 minutes or until light brown. Cool on cookie sheet for 1 minute. Remove to wire rack to cool completely. Yield: 5 1/2 dozen.

Barbara Gaylor, Michigan

PECAN FROSTIES

½ c. butter, softened
1¼ c. packed brown sugar
1 egg
1 tsp. vanilla extract
2 c. flour
½ tsp. soda
¼ tsp. salt
½ c. chopped pecans
2 tbsp. sour cream

Cream butter and 1 cup brown sugar in bowl until light and fluffy. Add egg and vanilla; mix well. Add mixture of flour, soda and salt gradually, mixing well after each addition. Shape into 1-inch balls; place 2 inches apart on ungreased cookie sheet. Combine pecans, ¼ cup brown sugar and sour cream in bowl. Make shallow depression in center of each cookie; fill with 1 teaspoon pecan filling. Bake at 350 degrees for 10 minutes or until brown. Cool on wire rack. Yield: 3 dozen.

Mandy McNealy, Indiana

◆◆◆◆◆◆◆◆◆◆◆◆◆◆◆◆◆◆◆◆◆◆◆◆◆◆◆◆◆

Hint: *To avoid overbaking, remove cookies from hot cookie sheet immediately unless otherwise instructed.*

◆◆◆◆◆◆◆◆◆◆◆◆◆◆◆◆◆◆◆◆◆◆◆◆◆◆◆◆◆

EASY PEPPERMINT BARS

1 roll refrigerator cookie dough,
    any flavor
2 egg whites
½ c. sugar
⅛ tsp. peppermint flavoring
2 tbsp. crushed peppermint stick candy

Slice cookie dough ¼ inch thick. Place overlapping slices in greased 9-inch square baking pan. Bake at 350 degrees for 15 minutes. Cookie layer will be puffy. Beat egg whites in bowl until foamy. Add sugar gradually, beating until stiff peaks form. Stir in flavoring. Spread over baked layer. Sprinkle with candy. Bake for 10 minutes longer. Cool. Cut into bars.

Cara Sue Smith, Arkansas

LEMON-GLAZED PERSIMMON BARS

1 egg
1 c. sugar
½ c. oil

1 8-oz. package dates, finely chopped
2½ tbsp. lemon juice
1 tsp. soda
1 c. persimmon pulp
1¾ c. flour
½ tsp. salt
1 tsp. each cinnamon, nutmeg
¼ tsp. cloves
1 c. chopped walnuts
1 c. confectioners' sugar

Combine first 4 ingredients in bowl; mix well. Blend 1½ teaspoons lemon juice and soda into persimmon pulp. Combine flour, salt and spices. Add persimmon pulp to date mixture alternately with flour mixture, mixing well after each addition. Stir in walnuts. Spread in greased and floured 10x15-inch baking pan. Bake at 350 degrees for 25 minutes or until light brown. Cool for 5 minutes. Combine 2 tablespoons lemon juice and confectioners' sugar in bowl; mix well. Spread over baked layer. Cool. Cut into bars.
Note: Omit lemon juice from batter when using frozen persimmon pulp.

Clara Sampson, California

PFEFFERNUESSE

¾ c. sugar
¼ c. milk
⅔ c. light corn syrup
¼ c. lard
¼ tsp. each salt and pepper
¼ tsp. each cloves, cardamom
½ tsp. each cinnamon, nutmeg
½ tsp. baking powder
¼ tsp. anise extract
½ tsp. vanilla extract
1 egg, beaten
4 c. (about) flour
Confectioners' sugar

Combine sugar, milk, corn syrup, lard, salt, pepper and spices in saucepan. Bring to a boil. Cool. Add baking powder, flavorings, egg and enough flour to make very stiff dough. Press into 8-inch cake pan. Chill, covered, for overnight to 2 weeks. Shape into ¼-inch thick ropes on surface dusted with confectioners' sugar. Cut into ¼-inch pieces on lightly greased baking sheet. Separate pieces. Bake at 350 degrees for 12 minutes or until light brown. Cool on paper towels; separate pieces. Let stand overnight. Store in airtight containers.
Note: Flavor improves with age. This traditional holiday treat is a welcome repeat gift. The cookies resemble crunchy spicy nuts.

Sharon Ireton, Idaho

PINEAPPLE-COCONUT DELIGHT

1 c. coconut
1   14-oz. can crushed pineapple
½ c. shortening
¾ c. sugar
2 eggs, slightly beaten
2 c. flour
1 tsp. baking powder
½ tsp. each soda, salt

Mix coconut and ¾ cup pineapple in bowl; set aside. Cream shortening, sugar and eggs in bowl until light and fluffy. Sift in dry ingredients; mix well. Add remaining pineapple; mix well. Pour into greased 10x15-inch baking pan. Spoon coconut mixture over top. Bake at 375 degrees for 25 minutes or until golden. Cool. Cut into squares.

Patricia A. Pavel, Pennsylvania

PINEAPPLE-LEMON DROPS

½ c. shortening
2 eggs
1   3-oz. package lemon gelatin
1 pkg. pound cake mix
1   8-oz. can crushed pineapple,
    well drained

Cream shortening and eggs in mixer bowl until light and fluffy. Blend in gelatin powder. Add half the cake mix. Beat at medium speed until fluffy. Add remaining cake mix. Beat at low speed until blended. Stir in pineapple. Drop by rounded teaspoonfuls 2 inches apart onto ungreased cookie sheet. Bake at 375 degrees for 10 minutes or until light brown. Cool on cookie sheet for 1 to 2 minutes or until firm. Remove to wire rack to cool completely. Yield: 4 dozen.

Malinda Chavez, California

PRUNE DROPS

2 c. sugar
1 c. shortening
3 eggs
1 c. chopped cooked prunes
3 c. sifted flour
1 tsp. soda
½ tsp. each salt, allspice
1 tsp. cinnamon
¼ tsp. each nutmeg, cloves
¾ c. chopped walnuts

Combine sugar, shortening, eggs and prunes in bowl; mix well. Sift in dry ingredients ⅓ at a time, mixing well after each addition. Stir in walnuts. Drop by teaspoonfuls 2 inches apart onto greased cookie sheet. Bake at 375 degrees for 12 minutes or until light brown. Cool on wire rack. Yield: 6 dozen.

Sharon J. Barreto, California

PISTACHIO SQUARES

1 c. butter, softened
½ c. sugar
1 egg
1 tsp. vanilla extract
1 c. flour
½ tsp. baking powder
¼ tsp. salt
½ c. milk
⅓ c. flaked coconut
6 tbsp. chopped pistachio nuts
1 c. vanilla-flavored
    confectioners' sugar frosting

Cream butter and sugar in bowl until light and fluffy. Add egg and vanilla; mix well. Add mixture of flour, baking powder and salt alternately with milk, mixing well after each addition. Add coconut and half the pistachio nuts. Spread in greased 9-inch square baking pan. Bake at 350 degrees for 20 minutes. Cool. Frost with vanilla frosting. Sprinkle with remaining nuts. Cut into squares.

Susan Hodges, Texas

POTATO CHIP COOKIES

1 c. margarine, softened
1 c. packed brown sugar
1 c. sugar
2 eggs
1 tsp. vanilla extract
2 c. crushed potato chips
1   6-oz. package butterscotch chips
2½ c. flour
1 tsp. baking powder

Cream margarine and sugars in bowl until light and fluffy. Add eggs and vanilla. Stir in potato chips, butterscotch chips and sifted dry ingredients. Drop by teaspoonfuls onto greased cookie sheet. Bake at 350 degrees for 10 minutes or until brown. Cool on wire rack. Yield: 6 dozen.

Pam Dunn, Oklahoma

◆◆◆◆◆◆◆◆◆◆◆◆◆◆◆◆◆◆◆◆◆◆◆◆◆◆◆◆

Hint: *To maintain shape, cookies should be completely cooled before storing in containers.*

◆◆◆◆◆◆◆◆◆◆◆◆◆◆◆◆◆◆◆◆◆◆◆◆◆◆◆◆

PUMPKIN BARS

4 eggs
1⅔ c. sugar
1 c. oil
1   16-oz. can pumpkin
2 c. flour
2 tsp. baking powder
1 tsp. each soda, salt
2 tsp. cinnamon
½ c. butter, softened
1   3-oz. package cream cheese, softened
1 tsp. vanilla extract
2 c. confectioners' sugar

Combine first 4 ingredients in bowl. Beat until light. Stir in mixture of flour, baking powder, soda, salt and cinnamon. Pour into greased 10x15-inch baking pan. Bake at 350 degrees for 30 minutes. Cool. Cream butter, cream cheese, vanilla and confectioners' sugar in bowl until light and fluffy. Spread over pumpkin layer. Cut into bars.

Barbara Borton, Washington

FROSTED PUMPKIN COOKIES

¾ c. shortening
1 c. sugar
1⅓ c. packed brown sugar
½ tsp. salt
3 c. flour
2 tsp. soda
½ tsp. nutmeg
1 tsp. cinnamon
¼ tsp. ginger
1 tsp. baking powder
2 c. canned pumpkin
¼ c. butter
¼ c. milk
1 tsp. vanilla extract
Confectioners' sugar

Cream shortening, sugar and 1 cup brown sugar in large bowl until light and fluffy. Sift next 7 ingredients together. Add to creamed mixture alternately with pumpkin, beating well after each addition. Drop by spoonfuls onto lightly greased cookie sheet. Bake at 350 degrees for 12 minutes. Cool on wire rack. Mix butter, milk and ⅓ cup brown sugar in saucepan. Bring to a boil. Remove from heat. Stir in vanilla. Cool slightly. Add enough confectioners' sugar to make of desired consistency. Frost cooled cookies. Yield: 6 dozen.

Roberta Stober, Ohio

RAISIN-FILLED COOKIES

1½ c. sugar
1 tbsp. flour
1 c. raisins
⅓ c. chopped walnuts
½ c. butter, softened
1 egg
½ c. milk
1 tsp. vanilla extract
3½ c. flour
2 tsp. cream of tartar
1 tsp. soda

Combine ½ cup sugar, 1 tablespoon flour and ½ cup water in saucepan. Cook until thickened, stirring constantly. Stir in raisins and walnuts. Cream butter and 1 cup sugar in bowl until light and fluffy. Add egg, milk and vanilla; mix well. Add mixture of 3½ cups flour, cream of tartar and soda gradually; mix well. Roll ⅛ inch thick on floured surface. Cut with cookie cutter. Place half the cookies on greased cookie sheet; spread 1 teaspoon filling over each. Top with remaining cookies; seal edges. Prick tops with fork. Bake at 425 degrees for 10 minutes. Cool on wire rack. Yield: 3-3½ dozen.

Laura Goller, West Virginia

PERFECT RAISIN DROP COOKIES

2 c. raisins
1 tsp. soda
2 c. sugar
1 c. shortening
1 tsp. vanilla extract
3 eggs, beaten
4 c. flour
1 tsp. baking powder
½ tsp. salt
1 tsp. cinnamon
¼ tsp. nutmeg
1 c. chopped walnuts

Cook raisins in 1 cup water in saucepan for 5 minutes. Cool. Add soda. Let stand for 5 minutes. Drain, reserving liquid. Cream sugar and shortening in bowl until light and fluffy. Add vanilla, eggs and reserved liquid; mix well. Sift in flour, baking powder, salt, cinnamon and nutmeg; mix well. Stir in walnuts and raisins. Drop by teaspoonfuls onto greased cookie sheet. Bake at 375 degrees for 13 minutes. Cool on wire rack. Store in airtight container. Yield: 9 dozen.

Elizabeth A. Shea, Florida

GOLDEN RAISIN WHIRLS

1 c. sugar
2 tbsp. cornstarch
1 c. light raisins, ground
1 tsp. grated lemon rind
¼ c. butter, softened
1   3-oz. package cream cheese, softened
1 egg
1 tbsp. lemon juice
1¾ c. flour
½ tsp. salt
¼ tsp. soda

Combine ⅓ cup sugar and cornstarch in saucepan. Stir in ⅓ cup water and raisins. Cook over medium heat until thickened, stirring constantly. Stir in lemon rind. Cool. Cream butter, cream cheese and ⅔ cup sugar in bowl until light and fluffy. Add egg and lemon juice; mix well. Stir in mixture of flour, salt and soda. Divide into 2 portions. Roll each portion into 7x11-inch rectangle on lightly floured surface. Spread with raisin filling. Roll as for jelly roll from long side; pinch edges to seal. Wrap in plastic wrap. Chill in refrigerator. Cut into ¼-inch slices. Place on greased cookie sheet. Bake at 375 degrees for 10 minutes or until light brown. Cool on wire rack. Yield: 7 dozen.

Catherine Carter, Illinois

SPICY RAISIN BARS

1 c. sifted flour
½ tsp. each soda, salt
1 tsp. pumpkin pie spice
½ c. shortening
½ c. packed brown sugar
1 tsp. vanilla extract
¼ c. milk
1 c. oats
1 c. raisins

Sift flour, soda, salt and spice into mixer bowl. Add shortening, brown sugar, vanilla and milk. Beat for 2 minutes or until smooth. Stir in oats and raisins. Spread in greased 7x11-inch baking dish. Bake at 350 degrees for 20 minutes or until firm. Cool. Cut into bars.

Photograph for this recipe on page 13.

COOL RAISIN CARDS

¾ c. shortening
1 c. packed light brown sugar
1 egg
¼ c. honey
2¼ c. sifted flour
1 tsp. soda
¾ tsp. salt
½ tsp. cinnamon
¼ tsp. each cloves, nutmeg
¾ c. chopped California raisins
2 tsp. cocoa
Several drops of red food coloring
1 c. sifted confectioners' sugar
1½ tbsp. melted butter
¼ tsp. vanilla extract
3 to 4 tsp. milk
Whole raisins

Cream shortening, brown sugar, egg and honey in bowl until light and fluffy. Sift in flour, soda and salt; mix well. Reserve ½ cup dough. Add spices and chopped raisins to remaining dough; mix well. Chill all dough for several minutes. Roll larger portion to ¼-inch thickness on floured surface; cut into 3¼x5-inch rectangles. Place 1 inch apart on lightly greased cookie sheet. Bake at 400 degrees for 10 minutes. Cool on wire rack. Divide reserved dough into 2 portions. Mix cocoa into 1 portion, roll as above and cut with small club and spade cutters. Mix food coloring into remaining dough, roll as above and cut with diamond and heart cutters. Place on greased cookie sheet. Bake for 5 minutes. Cool. Blend confectioners' sugar, butter, vanilla and enough milk to make thin frosting in bowl. Frost cookies; decorate with symbols and raisins to resemble cards. Yield: 9 cookies.

Esther Peeling, Pennsylvania

RASPBERRY BARS

1¾ c. flour
1 tsp. baking powder
½ c. plus 3 tbsp. butter
2 eggs
1 tbsp. milk
1 c. raspberry jam
1 c. sugar
2 c. coconut
1 tsp. vanilla extract

Combine flour and baking powder in bowl. Cut in ½ cup butter until crumbly. Add 1 egg and milk; mix well. Press into greased 8x12-inch baking pan. Spread jam over dough. Combine 3 tablespoons butter, sugar, 1 egg, coconut and vanilla in bowl; mix well. Spread over jam. Bake at 350 degrees for 130 minutes or until light lbrown. Cool. Cut into bars.

Nan Sulser, Texas

Recipes on pages 20, 21, 81, 85. ◆

RASPBERRY CHEWS

1½ c. unbleached flour
1½ c. oats
1 c. coconut
1 c. chopped pecans
1 c. packed brown sugar
½ c. butter, softened
2 10-oz. packages frozen red
  raspberries, thawed
2½ tbsp. cornstarch
½ tsp. lemon juice

Combine flour, oats, coconut, pecans, brown sugar, butter and 2 tablespoons water in bowl; mix well. Press half the mixture over bottom of greased 9x13-inch baking pan. Mix raspberries and cornstarch in saucepan. Cook for 2 minutes or until thickened, stirring constantly. Cool. Stir in lemon juice. Pour over prepared crust. Sprinkle with remaining oats mixture. Bake at 350 degrees for 35 minutes or until light brown. Cool. Cut into squares.

Tina Lehman, Tennessee

RHUBARB BARS

3 tbsp. cornstarch
3 c. chopped rhubarb
1½ c. sugar
1 tsp. vanilla extract
1½ c. oats
1½ c. flour
1 c. packed brown sugar
½ tsp. soda
1 c. shortening
½ c. chopped nuts

Dissolve cornstarch in ¼ cup cold water in saucepan. Add rhubarb, sugar and vanilla. Cook over medium heat until thickened, stirring occasionally. Combine remaining ingredients in bowl; mix until crumbly. Pat ¾ of the flour mixture into greased 9x13-inch baking pan. Top with rhubarb mixture. Sprinkle with remaining crumbs. Bake at 375 degrees for 30 minutes. Cool. Cut into bars.

Rita Poncelet, South Dakota

SANDBAKKLES

1 c. butter, softened
9 tbsp. sugar
½ tsp. vanilla extract
1 egg
2½ c. flour

Cream butter and sugar in bowl until light and fluffy. Add vanilla and egg; mix well. Blend in flour. Press ⅛ inch thick into sandbakkle molds. Place on ungreased cookie sheet. Bake at 400 degrees for 8 minutes or until light brown. Remove cookies from molds. Yield: 3½ dozen.

Lou Ann Restad, Minnesota

SCOTTISH SHORTBREAD

1 c. confectioners' sugar
3 c. flour
1 c. cornstarch
1 lb. butter

Sift dry ingredients into bowl. Cut in butter until crumbly. Knead until mixture forms smooth ball. Roll ¼ inch thick on lightly floured surface; cut as desired. Place on ungreased cookie sheet. Bake at 350 degrees for 13 minutes. Cool on wire rack. Yield: 3-4 dozen.

Judy Wright, Ontario, Canada

WHOLE WHEAT SHORTBREAD

⅓ c. packed brown sugar
1¼ c. whole wheat or graham flour
½ tsp. salt
½ c. butter
¼ c. sugar

Mix brown sugar, flour and salt in bowl. Cut in butter until crumbly. Knead until mixture forms smooth ball. Press into greased fluted shortbread mold. Score into 8 triangles. Chill for 1 hour. Bake at 300 degrees for 45 minutes or until firm and very lightly browned. Sprinkle half the sugar over top. Cool in pan for 5 minutes. Invert on wire rack. Sprinkle with remaining sugar. Cool completely. Break into triangles.

Brenda Foley, Wisconsin

SNICKERDOODLES

½ c. butter, softened
½ c. shortening
1½ c. sugar
2 eggs
2¾ c. flour
1 tsp. salt
2 tsp. cream of tartar
Cinnamon-sugar

Cream butter, shortening and sugar in bowl until light and fluffy. Beat in eggs. Add mixture of flour, salt and cream of tartar; mix well. Shape into balls. Roll in cinnamon-sugar. Place on ungreased cookie sheet. Bake at 400 degrees for 8 minutes or until light brown. Yield: 5 dozen.

Patricia Evans, Oklahoma

◆ *Recipes on pages 80, 90, 91.*

PIONEER SOURDOUGH COOKIES

½ c. butter, softened
¼ c. shortening
1¼ c. sugar
3 eggs
1 c. honey
2 c. Sourdough Starter
6 c. flour
1 tsp. nutmeg
4 tsp. soda
1 tsp. vanilla extract
Grated rind of 1 lemon (opt.)

Cream butter, shortening and sugar in bowl until light and fluffy. Add eggs and honey; mix well. Stir in Sourdough Starter, flour, nutmeg and soda. Add vanilla and lemon rind; mix well. Roll on lightly floured surface. Cut as desired. Place on ungreased cookie sheet. Bake at 375 degrees for 10 minutes. Cool on wire rack. Yield: 8 dozen.

Sourdough Starter — Dissolve 1 package yeast in 1 cup warm water in bowl. Stir in 1 cup flour. Refrigerate for 4 days. Feed with ¼ cup sugar, 1 cup flour and 1 cup milk on 5th day. Refrigerate for 5 days longer. Use for cooking on 10th day. Feed remaining starter as directed to retain for future use.

Judy Hogsett, West Virginia

SOUR CREAM COOKIES

1 c. butter, softened
2 c. sugar
3 eggs, beaten
1 c. sour cream
1 tsp. soda
2 c. flour
½ tsp. salt
1 tsp. baking powder

Cream butter and sugar in bowl until light and fluffy. Add eggs; mix well. Add sour cream and soda alternately with sifted dry ingredients, mixing well after each addition. Roll on floured surface; cut as desired. Sprinkle with additional sugar. Place on ungreased cookie sheet. Bake at 350 degrees until brown. Cool on wire rack. Yield: 3 dozen.

Maria Rayborn, Illinois

NATURAL SPICE COOKIES

¾ c. light molasses
½ c. oil
¼ c. sugar
1 egg
2 c. rye flour
¼ c. soy flour
¼ c. whole wheat flour
3 tbsp. nonfat dry milk powder
1 tsp. each ginger, cinnamon
½ tsp. salt

Combine first 4 ingredients in bowl. Beat until light and fluffy. Mix flours, milk powder and seasonings. Add to molasses mixture; mix well. Chill in refrigerator. Shape into 1-inch balls. Roll in additional sugar. Place on greased cookie sheet. Flatten with glass dipped in sugar. Bake at 350 degrees for 10 minutes or until firm. Cool on wire rack. Yield: 3 dozen.

Kristin Allen, Pennsylvania

EASTER BONNET COOKIES

1 c. Mazola margarine, softened
⅔ c. sugar
½ c. Karo light corn syrup
1 tbsp. lemon juice
2 eggs
3½ c. flour
2 recipes Decorator's Frosting
Paste food coloring

Cream first 5 ingredients in bowl until light and fluffy. Add flour gradually, beating until blended after each addition. Chill, covered, overnight. Roll ⅓ at a time to ⅛-inch thickness on lightly floured surface. Cut 30 cookies with 3½-inch scalloped round cookie cutter. Shape remaining dough by teaspoonfuls into balls. Place cookies and balls on ungreased cookie sheet. Bake at 350 degrees for 10 minutes. Cool on wire rack. Attach balls to centers of round cookies with a small amount of frosting. Tint half the remaining frosting as desired. Thin with enough water to make glaze. Brush over cookies. Tint remaining frosting. Spoon into pastry bag fitted with small decorator tip. Decorate cookies to resemble bonnets.

Decorator's Frosting

1   16-oz. package confectioners' sugar
3 egg whites
½ tsp. cream of tartar

Combine all ingredients in mixer bowl. Beat at low speed until blended. Beat at high speed for 7 minutes or until very stiff. Cover with damp cloth. Yield: 2 cups.

Photograph for this recipe on page 88.

FRUITY SUGAR COOKIES

¾ c. shortening
1 c. sugar
1 3-oz. package flavored gelatin
2 eggs
3 c. flour
1 tsp. each baking powder, salt

Cream shortening, sugar and gelatin in bowl until light and fluffy. Add eggs; mix well. Add sifted dry ingredients; mix well. Roll ¼ inch thick on floured surface. Cut with 3-inch cookie cutter. Place on greased cookie sheet. Bake at 375 degrees for 6 minutes or until light brown. Cool on wire rack. Yield: 3 dozen.

Rose Baley, California

SOUR CREAM SUGAR COOKIES

1 c. shortening
1¾ c. sugar
1 tsp. salt
1 tsp. lemon extract
2 eggs
¾ c. sour cream
1 tsp. soda
5 c. (or more) flour

Cream shortening and sugar in bowl until light and fluffy. Beat in salt and flavoring. Add eggs; mix well. Add sour cream mixed with soda; mix well. Add 4 cups flour ¼ at a time, mixing well after each addition. Knead on floured surface, adding enough flour to make stiff dough. Roll and cut as desired. Sprinkle with additional sugar. Place on greased cookie sheet. Bake at 350 degrees until light brown. Cool on wire rack. Yield: 7-8 dozen.

Mrs. Ed Luetkemeyer, Oklahoma

SUGARLESS COOKIES

1 c. unbleached flour
1 tsp. baking powder
¼ tsp. salt
½ c. butter, softened
1 egg
2 tsp. vanilla extract
1 c. coconut
½ c. finely chopped dates
½ c. raisins
1 c. finely chopped walnuts

Combine flour, baking powder and salt in bowl. Cut in butter until crumbly. Add egg and vanilla; mix well. Stir in coconut, dates, raisins and walnuts. Chill for 1 hour. Shape into 1-inch balls. Place ½ inch apart on greased cookie sheet; flatten cookies. Bake at 350 degrees for 15 minutes or until golden brown. Cool on wire rack. Yield: 2-3 dozen.

Helen Totura, Maryland

SUGARLESS OATMEAL COOKIES

2 eggs
½ c. oil
½ c. milk
1 tsp. vanilla extract
1 tbsp. baking powder
1 tsp. cinnamon
2 tsp. liquid sugar substitute
½ tsp. salt substitute
¾ c. flour
½ c. raisins
2 c. quick-cooking oats
Chopped nuts (opt.)

Combine eggs, oil, milk, vanilla, baking powder, cinnamon, sugar substitute and salt substitute in bowl; mix well. Beat in flour. Add raisins, oats and nuts; mix well. Drop by spoonfuls onto floured cookie sheet. Bake at 350 degrees for 25 minutes. Cool on wire rack. Yield: 3 dozen.

Wilma Voorhis, Ohio

SUGARLESS PEANUT BUTTER COOKIES

¼ c. diet margarine
8 env. Sweet N' Low
½ c. peanut butter
1 egg
⅓ c. milk
1 tsp. vanilla extract
1 c. flour
¼ tsp. salt
1 tsp. baking powder

Cream margarine, sweetener and peanut butter in bowl. Mix in egg, milk and vanilla. Sift in flour, salt and baking powder; mix well. Drop by spoonfuls onto foil-lined cookie sheet. Flatten with fork. Bake at 375 degrees for 10 minutes. Cool on wire rack. Yield: 3 dozen.

Mendie Adam, Oklahoma

◆◆◆◆◆◆◆◆◆◆◆◆◆◆◆◆◆◆◆◆◆◆◆◆◆◆◆◆◆

Hint: *To correct rolled or dropped cookie dough which is too dry, add 1 or 2 tablespoons softened butter or cream.*

◆◆◆◆◆◆◆◆◆◆◆◆◆◆◆◆◆◆◆◆◆◆◆◆◆◆◆◆◆

OLD-FASHIONED TEACAKES

1 c. butter, softened
2 c. sugar
2 eggs, beaten
5 c. flour
1 tsp. baking powder
1 tsp. nutmeg
1 tsp. soda
⅓ c. milk
⅓ c. (about) orange juice

Cream butter and sugar in bowl until light and fluffy. Add eggs; beat well. Sift flour, baking powder and nutmeg together. Dissolve soda in milk. Add to creamed mixture alternately with dry ingredients, beating well after each addition. Stir in enough orange juice to make soft dough. Roll to desired thickness on floured surface. Cut as desired. Place on greased cookie sheet. Bake at 350 degrees for 15 minutes or until light brown. Cool on wire rack. Store in airtight container. Yield: 7 dozen.

Barbara Thomas, Texas

TOFFEE SQUARES

½ c. melted butter
1 c. packed light brown sugar
1 egg, separated
2 c. sifted flour
½ tsp. soda
2 tsp. vanilla extract
1½ c. confectioners' sugar
3 tbsp. butter, softened
2 tbsp. cocoa
Chopped nuts (opt.)

Blend melted butter and brown sugar in bowl. Add beaten egg yolk, flour, soda and 1 teaspoon vanilla; mix well. Pat into rectangle on ungreased cookie sheet. Bake at 350 degrees for 12 minutes or until brown. Combine egg white, confectioners' sugar, softened butter, cocoa and remaining 1 teaspoon vanilla in bowl. Spread over hot baked layer. Sprinkle with nuts. Cool. Cut into squares.

Pat Lenz, Illinois

TUTTI-FRUTTI SQUARES

1 1-layer package cake mix
2 tbsp. butter, melted
1 tsp. vinegar
1 8-oz. package cream cheese, softened
1 egg
2 tbsp. sugar
½ c. flaked coconut

½ c. chopped pecans
¼ c. chopped maraschino cherries
½ c. well drained crushed pineapple
¾ c. semisweet miniature chocolate chips

Measure 1½ cups cake mix into bowl. Stir in butter, 1 tablespoon water and vinegar; mix well. Pat into greased 9-inch square pan. Bake at 350 degrees for 12 minutes or until firm and light brown around edges. Cool for 10 minutes. Combine cream cheese, egg and sugar in small bowl. Stir in coconut, pecans and cherries; spread over cooled layer. Mix pineapple with remaining cake mix. Add chocolate chips. Crumble over cream cheese layer. Bake at 350 degrees for 30 minutes or until light brown. Cool. Chill until serving time. Cut into squares.

June Richards, Kansas

VIENNESE FINGER COOKIES

1¼ c. butter, softened
1½ c. sifted confectioners' sugar
2 c. sifted flour
1 tbsp. orange juice
2 tsp. grated orange rind
⅛ tsp. vanilla extract
6 oz. semisweet chocolate, melted

Cream 1 cup butter and ½ cup confectioners' sugar in bowl until light and fluffy. Add flour, orange juice and rind; beat until smooth. Force 2-inch fingers through cookie press with star plate onto greased cookie sheet. Bake at 350 degrees for 10 to 15 minutes or until pale golden and firm to touch. Cool on cookie sheet for 5 minutes. Remove to wire rack to cool completely. Cream ¼ cup butter, 1 cup confectioners' sugar and vanilla in bowl until light and fluffy. Spread over half the cookies. Top with remaining cookies. Dip 1 end of each cookie in melted chocolate. Place on waxed paper. Yield: 2 dozen.

Louanne Dimmit, Texas

CHOCOLATE WAFFLE COOKIES

1 c. sugar
1½ c. flour
6 tbsp. cocoa
½ tsp. salt
3 eggs, beaten
14 tbsp. margarine, melted
2¾ tsp. vanilla extract
1½ c. confectioners' sugar
1½ tbsp. peanut butter

Combine first 5 ingredients, ¾ cup margarine and 1½ teaspoons vanilla in large bowl; mix well. Drop by teaspoonfuls onto medium-hot waffle iron. Bake for 55 to 60 seconds. Cool on wire rack. Combine confectioners' sugar, 2 tablespoons margarine, 1¼ teaspoons vanilla, peanut butter and 1 to 2 tablespoons hot water in bowl; mix well. Frost cooled cookies. Yield: 6 dozen.

Patricia Hyder, North Carolina

FRENCH WAFFLE COOKIES

6 eggs
3 sticks butter, softened
1½ c. plus 2 tbsp. packed brown sugar
¼ c. apricot Brandy
½ c. finely chopped pecans
4 c. sifted flour

Combine eggs, butter and brown sugar in mixer bowl. Beat at medium speed until smooth. Stir in Brandy and pecans. Add flour; mix well. Drop by heaping teaspoonfuls into center of each section of waffle iron. Bake for several minutes or until brown. Cool on wire rack. Store in airtight container. Yield: 4½ dozen.

Margaret Butler, California

WALNUT SWIRLS

1 c. flour
½ tsp. salt
1 c. unsalted butter, chilled
1 3-oz. package cream cheese, softened
6 oz. walnuts, finely ground
⅓ c. sugar
1 tsp. lemon juice
1 egg white, slightly beaten

Combine flour and salt in bowl. Cut in butter until crumbly. Add cream cheese. Mix with fork until smooth. Chill in refrigerator. Roll ½ at a time into 8x10-inch rectangles. Spread with mixture of remaining ingredients. Roll as for jelly roll; seal edges. Chill for 15 minutes. Cut into ¼-inch slices. Place on ungreased cookie sheet. Bake at 350 degrees for 15 minutes or until golden. Cool on wire rack. Yield: 6 dozen.

Lacey Saunders, Utah

WHEAT GERM FLORENTINES

¼ c. shortening, melted
⅔ c. toasted wheat germ
½ c. sugar
¼ c. flour
¼ tsp. salt

3 tbsp. whipping cream
1 tsp. vanilla extract
¼ c. finely chopped almonds
3 1-oz. squares semisweet chocolate, melted

Combine first 8 ingredients in bowl; mix well. Drop by scant teaspoonfuls onto lightly greased cookie sheet; flatten with spoon. Bake at 350 degrees for 7 minutes or until light brown. Cool for 2 minutes. Remove carefully to wire rack to cool completely. Spread cookie bottoms with chocolate. Let stand until chocolate is firm. Store between waxed paper. Yield: 3 dozen.

Janet Latham, Idaho

WINE COOKIES

1 c. butter, softened
2 c. sugar
2 egg yolks
5 c. sifted flour
Dash of salt
⅔ c. Sherry or Marsala
1 egg white, slightly beaten
Chopped nuts

Cream butter and sugar in bowl until light and fluffy. Add egg yolks; beat well. Add sifted dry ingredients alternately with wine, mixing well after each addition. Chill in refrigerator. Roll thinly on floured surface; cut with 2-inch cookie cutter. Place on ungreased cookie sheet. Brush with egg white; sprinkle with nuts. Bake at 325 degrees for 8 to 10 minutes. Cool on wire rack. Yield: 9 dozen.

Marcy Decker, Colorado

HERITAGE WINE COOKIES

1 c. butter, softened
2 c. sugar
3 eggs
1 tbsp. vanilla extract
¾ c. Sherry, Port or Madeira
Flour

Cream butter and sugar in bowl until light and fluffy. Add eggs and vanilla; mix well. Blend in wine. Add enough flour to make dough of consistency to roll as thin as knife blade. Cut into small cookies as desired. Place on ungreased cookie sheet. Bake at 350 degrees until golden. Cool on wire rack.
Note: These cookies will keep in airtight container in cool dry place for up to 1 year.

Maria Barela, Arizona

Candy Know-How

One of the most impressive ways to show off one's cooking ability is by candy-making. The recipes in this section include techniques that are simple enough for the beginner to prepare with ease, as well as those that will delight a master of candy-making. Depending upon your own cooking skills and confidence, you will find recipes to please all candy lovers.

Basic Guidelines for Candy-Making Success

- ◆ Read your recipe carefully to be sure you understand the desired result.

- ◆ Choose a cool, dry day for best results. If you must make candy on a humid day, be sure the cooking temperature is two degrees *higher than the recipe states to avoid sugary results.*

- ◆ Use a saucepan with 3 or 4 times the volume of the combined ingredients. This prevents messy boilovers. Use a saucepan with a heavy bottom or nonstick lining to prevent scorches.

- ◆ Grease the sides of the saucepan with a small amount of butter before you begin, then dissolve the sugar in the liquid before placing the saucepan over heat.

- ◆ Watch candy closely as it cooks! The temperature will rise slowly to the boiling point, then it will rise quite rapidly.

- ◆ Candies made with milk will scorch easily, so cook over medium heat. Candies made with water may be cooked over high heat.

◆ Unless your recipe states otherwise, never beat the candy mixture before it cools to 110 degrees. Do not move the saucepan or beat the mixture while hot or it will cause large sugar crystals to form, giving the candy a grainy texture.

◆ After the candy has cooled, cut or break up as instructed. Do not store until it is completely cold.

◆ Sugar absorbs moisture from the air, so it is best to store most candies in airtight containers (glass, ceramic or tin). Creamy candies (fudge, caramel, taffy) store better if pieces are individually wrapped in attractive foild or self-sealing transparent paper.

Using the Candy Thermometer

◆ Clip the candy thermometer on the side of the saucepan before starting. Be sure the bulb is completely covered with the syrup — not just boiling foam! Do not let the thermometer touch the bottom of the saucepan.

◆ When checking the thermometer reading, do not remove the saucepan from the heat or remove the thermometer from the syrup to check.

◆ When the desired temperature is reached, remove the thermometer then allow it to cool completely before washing it.

Candy Testing Chart

Candy	Cold Water Test ★	Temperature At Sea Level ★★
Fudge, Penuche, Fondant	Soft ball (can be picked up but flattens)	234 to 240 degrees
Caramels	Firm ball (holds shape unless pressed)	242 to 248 degrees
Divinity, Taffy, Caramel Corn	Hard-ball (holds shape though pliable)	250 to 268 degrees
Butterscotch, English Toffee	Soft crack (separates into hard threads but not brittle)	270 to 290 degrees
Brittles	Hard crack (separates into hard and brittle threads)	300 to 310 degrees

★　Drop about ½ teaspoon of boiling syrup into one cup water, and test firmness of mass with fingers.

★★　Subtract approximately 2 degrees for every 1,000 feet increase in altitude.

APRICOT CANDY

1 orange
1 lemon
1 lb. dried apricots
1¾ to 2 c. sugar
Chopped nuts
Confectioners' sugar

Squeeze juice from orange and lemon; set juice aside. Put apricots and orange and lemon rinds through food chopper. Combine with juices and sugar in saucepan. Cook for 15 minutes, stirring frequently. Stir in nuts. Cool completely. Shape into tiny balls; roll in confectioners' sugar. Place in paper bonbon cups. Yield: 2½ pounds.

Elsie Goad, Tennessee

FAVORITE PEANUT BRITTLE

2 c. sugar
1 c. light corn syrup
1 lb. raw peanuts
⅛ tsp. salt
1 tsp. vanilla extract
2 tbsp. butter
2 tsp. soda

Combine sugar, corn syrup and 1 cup water in saucepan. Cook to 270 to 290 degrees on candy thermometer, soft-crack stage. Stir in peanuts. Cook until golden brown. Add salt, vanilla and butter; mix well. Remove from heat. Stir in soda quickly. Spread on buttered surface. Cool. Break into pieces. Yield: 2½ pounds.

Jodie Dean, Utah

BURNT SUGAR CANDY

3 c. sugar
1½ c. half and half
Pinch of salt
½ c. butter
1 c. chopped nuts

Caramelize 1 cup sugar in saucepan. Bring half and half to the boiling point in saucepan. Remove from heat. Stir in caramelized sugar and remaining 2 cups sugar until completely dissolved. Cook, covered, over medium heat for 2 to 3 minutes or until steam washes sugar crystals from side of pan. Cook, uncovered, to 250 to 268 degrees on candy thermometer, hard-ball stage; do not stir. Add salt, butter and nuts. Beat until creamy. Pour onto buttered platter. Let stand until firm. Cut into pieces. Yield: 3 pounds.

Myrtle Sturgeon, California

MICROWAVE PEANUT BRITTLE

1 c. light corn syrup
2 c. sugar
⅔ c. peanuts
2 tbsp. butter
2 tsp. vanilla extract
2 tsp. soda

Combine first 3 ingredients in 3-quart glass casserole. Microwave on High for 12 minutes, turning casserole once. Stir in butter and vanilla. Microwave on High for 4 minutes. Stir in soda. Pour onto marble slab or large baking sheet. Cool. Break into pieces. Store in airtight container. Yield: 1½ pounds.

Katherine Robinson, Texas

SKILLET PEANUT BRITTLE

3 c. sugar
½ c. corn syrup
¼ c. butter
1 c. peanuts
1 tsp. soda
1 tsp. vanilla extract

Combine sugar, corn syrup and 1 cup water in heavy skillet. Cook to 300 to 310 degrees on candy thermometer, hard-crack stage. Stir in butter and peanuts. Cook over low heat to 300 degrees, stirring occasionally. Stir in soda and vanilla. Spread on 2 buttered baking sheets. Stretch as thin as possible as mixture cools. Break into pieces when completely cooled. Yield: 2 pounds.

Blossom E. Snively, California

WALNUT BRITTLE

½ c. maple syrup
2 c. packed light brown sugar
¼ c. butter
½ tsp. maple flavoring
1½ c. chopped walnuts
¼ tsp. soda

Bring maple syrup and ½ cup water to the boiling point in saucepan. Remove from heat. Stir in brown sugar until completely dissolved. Cook, covered, over high heat for 2 to 3 minutes or until steam washes sugar crystals from side of pan. Cook, uncovered, to 300 to 310 degrees on candy thermometer, hard-crack stage, stirring constantly. Stir in butter, flavoring, walnuts and soda. Spread in thin layer on buttered baking sheet. Cool. Break into pieces. Yield: 1½ pounds.

Jamie Fester, California

CARAMELS

2.c. sugar
1 c. light corn syrup
½ c. butter
1 can sweetened condensed milk

Combine sugar and corn syrup in heavy saucepan. Bring to a boil. Stir in butter. Add condensed milk gradually, stirring constantly. Cook for 15 minutes or to 230 degrees on candy thermometer, stirring constantly. Pour into buttered 8-inch square dish. Let stand until firm. Cut into squares.
Yield: 2 pounds.

Gordon Gee, West Virginia

BROWN SUGAR CARAMELS

1 c. melted butter
1   16-oz. package brown sugar
Dash of salt
1 c. light corn syrup
1 can sweetened condensed milk
1 tsp. vanilla extract

Blend first 4 ingredients in saucepan. Stir in condensed milk gradually. Cook over medium heat to 240 to 248 degrees on candy thermometer, firm-ball stage, stirring constantly. Stir in vanilla. Pour into buttered 9x9-inch dish; do not scrape bottom or side of pan. Let stand until firm. Cut into squares.
Yield: 3 pounds.

Valerie Riggs, Oklahoma

FUDGY CARAMELS

3 sq. unsweetened chocolate, melted
2 c. sugar
1 c. packed brown sugar
½ c. butter
⅛ tsp. salt
1 c. corn syrup
1 c. cream
1 tsp. vanilla extract

Combine first 7 ingredients in saucepan. Bring to the boiling point. Cook, covered, for 5 minutes. Cook, uncovered, to 240 to 248 degrees on candy thermometer, firm-ball stage, stirring constantly. Remove from heat. Stir in vanilla. Pour into buttered 6x10-inch dish; do not scrape bottom or side of pan. Let stand until firm. Cut into ¾-inch squares.
Yield: 3 pounds.

Lois Smith, Oregon

CARAMEL CREAM CANDY

½ c. light corn syrup
2 c. sugar
2 c. whipping cream
½ tsp. vanilla extract
½ c. chopped walnuts

Mix corn syrup, sugar and 1 cup cream in saucepan. Cook until creamy and golden, stirring constantly. Add remaining cream gradually, maintaining boiling point. Cook, covered, for 2 minutes or until steam washes sugar crystals from side of pan. Cook, uncovered, to 240 to 248 degrees on candy thermometer, firm-ball stage; do not stir. Cool to lukewarm, 110 degrees. Beat until creamy. Stir in vanilla and walnuts. Pour into buttered dish. Let stand until firm. Cut into squares. Yield: 3 pounds.

Wanda Nietfeld, Kansas

CHOCOLATE-PECAN CARAMELS

1   12-oz. package chocolate chips
2 tbsp. shortening
1   14-oz. package caramels
5 tbsp. butter
1 c. coarsely chopped pecans

Melt chocolate chips and shortening in double boiler, stirring until smooth; remove from heat. Spread half the chocolate in foil-lined 8-inch square dish. Chill for 15 minutes or until firm. Keep remaining chocolate warm. Combine caramels, butter and 2 tablespoons water in double boiler. Cook over boiling water until melted. Stir in pecans. Pour over chilled chocolate; spreading evenly. Chill for 15 minutes. Top with remaining warm chocolate; spread evenly. Chill for 1 hour. Cut into squares. Yield: 2 pounds.

Penny Welch, Iowa

MICROWAVE CARAMELS

1 c. melted maragarine
2 c. sugar
2 c. light corn syrup
2 c. whipping cream
1 tbsp. vanilla extract

Combine margarine, sugar, corn syrup and 1 cup cream in large glass bowl. Microwave on High for 20 minutes. Add remaining cream; mix well. Microwave for 12 to 14 minutes longer or to 240 degrees on candy thermometer, soft-ball stage. Stir in vanilla. Pour into buttered 9x13-inch dish; do not scrape bottom or side of pan. Let stand until firm. Cut into squares. Yield: 3 pounds.

Phyllis Scheuer, Illinois

CREAMY CARAMELS

2 c. packed light brown sugar
1 c. light corn syrup
½ c. margarine
2 c. whipping cream
1 c. pecans

Combine brown sugar, corn syrup and margarine in saucepan. Bring to the boiling point. Stir in cream gradually. Cook to 234 to 240 degrees on candy thermometer, soft-ball stage. Remove from heat. Stir in pecans. Pour into buttered 8x13-inch dish; do not scrape bottom or side of pan. Let stand until firm. Cut into squares. Yield: 3 pounds.

Sally Jo Marquis, Missouri

MOCHA PECAN CARAMELS

2 c. sugar
2 tsp. instant coffee powder
1 tsp. salt
1 c. light cream
½ c. light corn syrup
1½ c. butter
1 tsp. vanilla extract
1 c. coarsely chopped pecans

Combine sugar, coffee powder, salt, cream, corn syrup and butter in heavy 3-quart saucepan. Bring to the boiling point over medium heat, stirring constantly; reduce heat. Cook to 240 to 248 degrees on candy thermometer, firm-ball stage, stirring frequently. Cool for 5 minutes. Stir in vanilla and pecans. Pour into buttered 8-inch square dish; do not scrape bottom or side of pan. Let stand until firm. Cut into 1-inch squares. Wrap each in plastic wrap. Yield: 3 pounds.

Betty Bell, Alabama

CHOCOLATE GARNISHES

1   1-oz. bar semisweet or milk chocolate
4 oz. semisweet or milk chocolate
3   6-oz. packages semisweet chocolate chips
3 tbsp. shortening (opt.)
Fresh rose, lemon or mint leaves
Miniature paper muffin cup liners

Chocolate Curls—Microwave unwrapped 1-ounce semisweet or milk chocolate bar on High for 45 seconds or until chocolate feels warm to the touch. Draw vegetable peeler across underside of bar to form curls onto waxed paper-lined plate. Chill until firm. Store in covered container in refrigerator.

Chocolate Cut-Outs—Melt 4 ounces semisweet or milk chocolate in double boiler over hot water. Spread into 7-inch square on waxed paper-lined tray. Chill for 5 to 8 minutes or until chocolate begins to set. Press small cutters into chocolate to make imprint; do not remove cut-outs. Chill for several hours to overnight. Remove cut-outs. Store, tightly covered, in refrigerator.

Chocolate Leaves—Melt chocolate chips in double boiler over hot water. Add enough shortening to make of desired consistency. Wash fresh rose, lemon or mint leaves; pat dry. Spread ⅓ of the melted chocolate on undersides of leaves with small pastry brush; place on waxed paper-lined tray. Chill until firm. Peel green leaf away from chocolate leaf. Store in refrigerator.

Chocolate Cups—Paint inside of 1¾-inch paper liners in miniature muffin cups with ⅓ of the melted chocolate using pastry brush. Chill overnight. Peel paper from cups gently. Store, tightly covered, in refrigerator.

Chocolate Butterflies—Fill pastry bag fitted with small writing tip with remaining melted chocolate. Pipe into butterfly designs on 3-inch waxed paper squares. Let stand for 20 minutes or until chocolate begins to set. Lift wings 1 at a time with spatula; fold gently to resemble wings in flight. Place between cups of inverted egg carton to retain shape. Chill until firm. Store in refrigerator.

Photograph for this recipe on this page.

HARD CINNAMON CANDY

1½ c. light corn syrup
3¾ c. sugar
1 tsp. oil of cinnamon

Bring corn syrup and 1 cup water to a boil in saucepan. Remove from heat. Stir in sugar until completely dissolved. Cook, covered, over high heat for 2 minutes or until steam washes crystals from side of pan. Cook, uncovered, to 300 to 310 degrees on candy thermometer, hard-crack stage; do not stir. Add oil of cinnamon and red food coloring. Sprinkle foil-lined 12x24-inch pan with confectioners' sugar. Pour in candy; do not scrape bottom or side of pan. Let stand until completely cooled. Break into pieces.

Lisa Jennings, Oklahoma

DATE-PECAN ROLL

1 c. milk
2 c. sugar
1 c. chopped dates
¼ c. butter
½ c. chopped pecans
1 c. shredded coconut

Bring milk to the boiling point in saucepan; remove from heat. Stir in sugar until completely dissolved. Cook, covered, over medium-heat for 2 to 3 minutes or until steam washes sugar crystals from side of pan. Cook, uncovered, to 234 to 240 degrees on candy thermometer, soft-ball stage; do not stir. Add dates and butter. Cook until mixture forms ball, stirring constantly; remove from heat. Add pecans and half the coconut. Beat until stiff. Shape into 12-inch roll on moist cloth. Sprinkle with remaining coconut; roll in cloth. Let stand until firm. Cut into slices.

Marjolyn Bryan, West Virginia

HOLIDAY DIVINITY

3 c. sugar
¾ c. light corn syrup
¼ tsp. salt
1 3-oz. package any flavor gelatin
2 egg whites, stiffly beaten
1 tsp. vanilla extract
1 c. chopped nuts
½ c. coconut

Bring ¾ cup water to the boiling point in saucepan. Remove from heat. Add sugar, corn syrup and salt; mix until sugar is completely dissolved. Cook, covered, over high heat for 2 to 3 minutes or until steam washes sugar crystals from side of pan. Cook, uncovered, to 250 to 268 degrees on candy ther-mometer, hard-ball stage; do not stir. Add gelatin powder to egg whites gradually, beating constantly. Add hot syrup gradually, beating constantly. Beat at high speed until thickened. Add vanilla, nuts and coconut; mix well. Pour into buttered dish. Let stand until firm. Cut into squares. Yield: 2 pounds.

Carolyn Saxe, Illinois

CHOCOLATE KISS DIVINITY

2½ c. sugar
½ c. light corn syrup
¼ tsp. salt
2 egg whites
1 tsp. vanilla extract
½ c. chopped nuts
30 milk chocolate kisses

Combine sugar, corn syrup, salt and ½ cup water in 2-quart saucepan. Bring to a boil over medium heat, stirring constantly. Cook, covered, over high heat for 2 to 3 minutes or until steam washes sugar crystals from side of pan. Cook, uncovered, to 260 degrees on candy thermometer, hard-ball stage; do not stir. Add gradually to stiffly beaten egg whites, beating constantly at high speed until stiff peaks form. Beat in vanilla. Stir in nuts. Drop by teaspoonfuls onto waxed paper. Press chocolate kiss onto each. Cool. Store in airtight container. Yield: 2½ dozen.

Photograph for this recipe on Cover.

ELEGANT DIVINITY

2 c. sugar
½ c. light corn syrup
¼ tsp. salt
2 egg whites, stiffly beaten
1 tsp. vanilla extract
¾ c. chopped candied cherries

Bring ½ cup water to the boiling point in saucepan. Remove from heat. Add sugar, corn syrup and salt. Stir until sugar is completely dissolved. Cook, covered, over high heat for 2 to 3 minutes or until steam washes sugar crystals from side of pan. Cook, uncovered, to 240 to 248 degrees on candy thermometer, firm-ball stage; do not stir. Remove from heat. Add to egg whites gradually, beating constantly. Wipe sugar crystals from side of pan with damp cloth. Add vanilla; beat until mixture holds shape when dropped from spoon. Fold in cherries. Drop by spoonfuls onto waxed paper. Let stand until firm. Yield: 1 pound.

Luella Styles, Illinois

STRAWBERRY DIVINITY

3 c. sugar
¾ c. light corn syrup
1 3-oz. package strawberry gelatin
2 egg whites, stiffly beaten

Bring ¾ cup water to the boiling point in saucepan. Remove from heat. Add sugar and corn syrup. Stir until completely dissolved. Cook, covered, over high heat for 2 to 3 minutes or until steam washes sugar crystals from side of pan. Cook, uncovered, to 270 to 290 degrees on candy thermometer, soft-crack stage; do not stir. Add gelatin powder to egg whites gradually, beating constantly. Add hot syrup very gradually, beating constantly until very stiff. Drop by teaspoonfuls onto waxed paper. Cool until firm. Yield: 2 pounds.

May Leonhart, Oklahoma

MUDDY BOTTOM DIVINITY

2 8-oz. milk chocolate bars
2½ c. sugar
½ c. light corn syrup
¼ tsp. salt
2 egg whites, stiffly beaten
1 tsp. vanilla extract
½ c. pecans

Line 9x9-inch pan with foil. Foil should extend over edges. Arrange chocolate bars on foil. Bring ½ cup water to the boiling point in saucepan. Remove from heat. Add sugar, corn syrup and salt; stir until sugar is completely dissolved. Cook, covered, over high heat for 2 to 3 minutes or until steam washes sugar crystals from side of pan. Cook, uncovered, to 250 to 268 degrees on candy thermometer, hard-ball stage; do not stir. Pour hot syrup over egg whites gradually, beating constantly at high speed. Add vanilla. Beat for 4 to 5 minutes or until candy holds its shape. Stir in pecans. Spread evenly over chocolate bars. Cool. Lift foil to remove candy from pan. Cut into squares. Store in airtight container. Yield: 2 pounds.

Stacy Smith, Texas

UNCOOKED FONDANT

½ c. butter
1 16-oz. package confectioners' sugar
¼ c. whipping cream
¾ tsp. vanilla extract

Beat butter in bowl until soft and creamy. Add confectioners' sugar gradually, beating until very light. Add whipping cream and vanilla; mix well. Knead until smooth. Shape into 1-inch balls; roll in additional confectioners' sugar. Chill until firm.

Store, covered, in refrigerator. Fondant balls may be dipped in chocolate if desired. Yield: 1 pound.

Joyce Boyce, Arkansas

DIRECTIONS FOR BASIC FONDANT

Bring 1 cup water to the boiling point in heavy saucepan. Remove from heat. Add 3 cups sugar; stir until sugar is completely dissolved. Place over medium heat. Sprinkle in 1/16 teaspoon cream of tartar by tapping spoon on edge of pan. Syrup will boil up and must be stirred down. Cook, covered, for 2 to 3 minutes or until steam washes sugar crystals from side of pan. Cook, uncovered, to 234 degrees on candy thermometer, soft-ball stage; do not stir. Pour onto marble slab sprinkled with ice water; do not scrape pan. Let stand until cool enough to retain fingerprint momentarily. Work with candy scraper or wooden spoon by lifting and folding edges to center until candy becomes opaque and creamy. Dust hands with confectioners' sugar. Knead for several minutes. Let ripen in tightly covered container in cool place for 24 hours or longer. Place in double boiler. Heat gradually over 180-degree water until fondant can be shaped. Place on marble slab. Color and flavor if desired by making several slashes in fondant, adding food coloring and flavoring; slash and fold repeatedly until well mixed. Add nuts, candied fruit or coconut in the same manner if desired. Shape into ½-inch ropes; cut as desired. Dip fondant at room temperature into favorite chocolate coating.

Variations:
Coffee Fondant — Replace water in Basic Fondant with strong coffee. Cook as directed.
Brown Sugar Fondant — Use brown sugar for half the sugar measurement in Basic Fondant. Cook as directed.
Maple Fondant — Use maple sugar for half the sugar measurement in Basic Fondant. Cook as directed.
Orange Fondant — Replace water with orange juice in Basic Fondant. Cook as directed.

EASY FUDGE

1 16-oz. package confectioners' sugar
½ c. nonfat dry milk powder
½ c. cocoa
Dash of salt
½ c. butter
½ c. chopped nuts

Sift first 4 ingredients into bowl. Combine butter and ⅓ cup water in saucepan. Bring to a boil. Stir into dry ingredients; mix well. Add nuts; mix well. Pour into buttered 8-inch square dish. Chill for several hours. Cut into squares. Yield: 1½ pounds.

Anne McCullen, North Carolina

CREAMY PEANUT BUTTER FUDGE

1   16-oz. package confectioners' sugar
½ c. milk
2 c. marshmallow creme
1 c. peanut butter

Blend confectioners' sugar and milk in saucepan. Bring to a boil over low heat. Boil for 2 minutes. Beat in marshmallow creme. Add peanut butter; blend well. Spread in buttered shallow pan. Chill until firm. Cut into squares. Yield: 2 pounds.

Dolores Wyatt, Tennessee

CREAMY FUDGE

¼ c. butter
2   1-oz. squares unsweetened chocolate
1 c. milk
2 c. sugar
½ c. chopped walnuts

Melt butter and chocolate over low heat in saucepan. Add milk. Bring to the boiling point. Remove from heat. Stir in sugar until completely dissolved. Cook, covered, over medium heat for 2 to 3 minutes or until steam washes sugar crystals from side of pan. Cook, uncovered, to 234 to 240 degrees on candy thermometer, soft-ball stage; do not stir. Cool to lukewarm, 110 degrees; do not stir. Beat until mixture thickens and loses its luster. Stir in walnuts. Pour into buttered dish. Let stand until firm. Cut into squares. Yield: 2 pounds.

Kristina Elliott, California

FANTASY FUDGE

1⅓ c. evaporated milk
1½ c. margarine
6 c. sugar
2   12-oz. packages semisweet
    chocolate chips
1   13-oz. jar marshmallow creme
2 c. chopped nuts
2 tsp. vanilla extract

Bring evaporated milk and margarine to the boiling point in saucepan. Remove from heat. Stir in sugar until completely dissolved. Cook, covered, over medium heat for 2 to 3 minutes or until steam washes sugar crystals from side of pan. Cook, uncovered, to 234 to 240 degrees on candy thermometer, soft-ball stage; do not stir. Remove from heat. Add chocolate chips. Stir until melted. Add marshmallow creme, nuts and vanilla. Beat until mixture thickens. Pour into 2 buttered 9x13-inch dishes. Let stand until firm. Cut into squares. Yield: 6 pounds.

Brenda Bryant, North Carolina

GERMAN CHOCOLATE FANCY FUDGE

2 sticks margarine, melted
1 lg. can evaporated milk
1 c. plus 2 tbsp. packed brown sugar
3 c. plus 6 tbsp. sugar
1 tbsp. vanilla extract
2 oz. German's sweet chocolate, chopped
1   12-oz. package semisweet
    chocolate chips
13 oz. milk chocolate candy, chopped
8 oz. marshmallows
2 c. chopped walnuts

Combine margarine and evaporated milk in saucepan. Bring to the boiling point. Remove from heat. Stir in sugars until completely dissolved. Cook over medium heat until mixture comes to the boiling point. Cook, covered, for 3 minutes. Remove from heat. Add vanilla, sweet chocolate, chocolate chips, milk chocolate, marshmallows and walnuts. Stir until chocolate melts and mixture thickens. Pour into buttered 10x15-inch dish. Chill until firm. Cut into squares. Yield: 6 pounds.

Audra Nigro, Illinois

PEANUT BUTTER MARBLED FUDGE

¾ c. butter
1 c. peanut butter
1   16-oz. package confectioners' sugar
½ c. chocolate chips

Melt butter in saucepan; remove from heat. Add peanut butter; beat well. Add confectioners' sugar; beat well. Add chocolate chips; mix until just marbleized. Pour into buttered 8-inch square dish. Chill overnight. Cut into squares. Yield: 2 pounds.

Phyllis Hall, Ohio

NO-FAIL MICROWAVE FUDGE

3 c. sugar
¾ c. margarine, softened
⅔ c. evaporated milk
1   12-oz. package semisweet
    chocolate chips
2 c. marshmallow creme
1 c. chopped nuts
1 tsp. vanilla extract

Combine sugar, margarine and evaporated milk in bowl; mix well. Microwave on High for 8 minutes, stirring several times. Add chocolate chips; stir until melted. Add remaining ingredients; mix well. Pour into buttered 9x13-inch dish. Let stand until firm. Cut into squares. Yield: 3 pounds.

Debra Bishop, Virginia

MICROWAVE PECAN FUDGE

2 c. sugar
1/3 c. cocoa
2/3 c. milk
2 tbsp. light corn syrup
1/4 tsp. salt
2 tbsp. margarine, softened
1 tsp. vanilla extract
1/2 c. chopped pecans

Combine first 5 ingredients in 3-quart glass casserole; mix well. Add margarine. Microwave on High for 5 minutes, stirring once. Microwave for 5 to 6 minutes longer or to 240 degrees on candy thermometer; do not stir. Cool to lukewarm, 110 degrees; do not stir. Add vanilla. Beat until thickened and mixture loses its luster. Stir in pecans. Pour into buttered 9-inch dish. Let stand until set. Cut into squares.
Yield: 1½ pounds.

Jan Flickinger, California

QUICK MICROWAVE FUDGE

1/2 c. (heaping) cocoa
1   16-oz. package confectioners' sugar, sifted
1/3 c. milk
1 stick butter, sliced
1 tsp. vanilla extract
1/2 c. chopped pecans (opt.)

Combine all ingredients except pecans in large glass bowl; mix well. Microwave on High for 3 minutes; mix well. Stir in pecans. Pour into buttered 8x8-inch dish. Chill for 30 minutes. Cut into squares.
Yield: 1½ pounds.

Kathleen Hanewinkel, Missouri

SUPER EASY MICROWAVE FUDGE

1   16-oz. package confectioners' sugar
1/2 c. cocoa
1/4 tsp. salt
1/4 c. milk
1 tbsp. vanilla extract
1/2 c. margarine, softened
1 c. chopped nuts

Combine first 5 ingredients in 1½-quart glass casserole; mix until partially blended. Dot with margarine. Microwave on High for 2 minutes. Mix until smooth. Stir in nuts. Spoon into 4x8-inch dish lined with waxed paper. Chill, covered, for 1 hour. Cut into squares. Yield: 1½ pounds.

Cindy Mathey, Virginia

EASY CREAMY COCOA FUDGE

1/2 c. butter, melted
3/4 c. cocoa
1 1/3 c. sweetened condensed milk
4½ c. sifted confectioners' sugar
2 tsp. vanilla extract
1 c. chopped nuts (opt.)

Blend butter and cocoa in saucepan. Stir in condensed milk. Bring to a boil over low heat, stirring constantly. Remove from heat. Add confectioners' sugar and vanilla; beat until smooth. Stir in nuts. Pour into foil-lined 9-inch square pan. Garnish with walnut halves. Cool. Cut into squares.
Yield: 2½ pounds.

Photograph for this recipe on Cover.

BUTTERMILK FUDGE

1 c. buttermilk
1 tsp. soda
1/4 c. light corn syrup
2 c. sugar
2 tbsp. butter
1 tsp. vanilla extract
1 c. chopped nuts

Combine buttermilk and soda in saucepan. Add corn syrup. Bring to the boiling point. Remove from heat. Stir in sugar until completely dissolved. Cook, covered, over medium heat for 2 to 3 minutes or until steam washes sugar crystals from side of pan. Cook, uncovered, to 234 to 240 degrees on candy thermometer, soft-ball stage; do not stir. Add butter and vanilla. Cool to lukewarm, 110 degrees; do not stir. Beat until mixture thickens and loses its luster. Stir in nuts. Pour into buttered dish. Let stand until firm. Cut into squares. Yield: 1½ pounds.

Sharon Richardson, Oklahoma

CHERRY CREME FUDGE

1 c. light cream
2 tbsp. light corn syrup
3 c. sugar
1/4 tsp. salt
1 tsp. vanilla extract
1/2 c. marshmallow creme
1/2 stick butter, sliced
3/4 c. coarsely chopped pecans
3/4 c. chopped red candied cherries

Combine cream and corn syrup in saucepan. Bring to the boiling point. Remove from heat. Stir in sugar and salt until completely dissolved. Cook, covered, over medium heat for 2 to 3 minutes or until steam washes sugar crystals from side of pan. Cook, uncovered, to 234 to 240 degrees on candy thermometer, soft-ball stage; do not stir. Remove from heat. Cool to lukewarm, 110 degrees; do not stir. Beat in vanilla, marshmallow creme and butter. Stir in pecans and cherries. Pour into buttered 8-inch square dish. Let stand until firm. Cut into squares. Yield: 2 pounds.

Patricia Mincks, Kansas

CHRISTMAS FUDGE

½ c. cream
½ c. milk
1 tbsp. light corn syrup
1⅔ c. sugar
⅓ c. packed light brown sugar
¼ tsp. salt
2 tbsp. butter
½ tsp. each almond, vanilla extract
⅔ c. chopped walnuts
½ c. chopped candied fruits
¼ c. chopped candied cherries

Combine cream, milk and corn syrup in saucepan. Bring to the boiling point. Remove from heat. Stir in sugars and salt until completely dissolved. Cook, covered, over low heat for 2 to 3 minutes or until steam washes sugar crystals from side of pan. Cook, uncovered, to 234 to 240 degrees on candy thermometer, soft-ball stage; do not stir. Remove from heat. Add butter and flavorings; do not stir. Cool to lukewarm, 110 degrees; do not stir. Beat until mixture thickens and loses its luster. Stir in walnuts and fruits. Pour into buttered 8-inch square dish. Let stand until firm. Cut into squares. Yield: 1½ pounds.

Louise Gibson, California

COCONUT FUDGE

3 c. sugar
1 c. evaporated milk
8 tsp. margarine
1   7-oz. jar marshmallow creme
1   12-oz. package flaked coconut
1 c. chopped nuts

Mix first 3 ingredients in saucepan. Bring to a boil, stirring frequently. Boil for 5 minutes, stirring constantly. Remove from heat. Add marshmallow creme; beat until creamy and smooth. Add coconut and nuts. Pour into buttered dish. Let stand until firm. Cut into squares. Yield: 2 pounds.

Martha Brown, Tennessee

COCONUT-WALNUT FUDGE

3 c. sugar
1   12-oz. package chocolate chips
2½ tbsp. finely shredded coconut
4 c. coarsely chopped walnuts

Bring ½ cup water to the boiling point in saucepan. Remove from heat. Add sugar; stir until completely dissolved. Cook, covered, over high heat for 2 to 3 minutes or until steam washes sugar crystals from side of pan. Cook, uncovered, to 234 to 240 degrees on candy thermometer, soft-ball stage; do not stir. Remove from heat. Add chocolate chips. Cool to lukewarm, 110 degrees; do not stir. Beat until mixture thickens and loses its luster. Stir in coconut and walnuts. Spread in foil-lined 9x13-inch dish. Chill until firm. Cut into squares. Store in refrigerator. Yield: 3 pounds.

Lisa Jones, North Carolina

NUTTY FUDGE

1 lg. can evaporated milk
1½ c. melted margarine
5 c. sugar
5 sq. unsweetened chocolate, melted
1   12-oz. package chocolate chips
1   7-oz. jar marshmallow creme
2 tsp. vanilla extract
2 c. chopped nuts (opt.)

Combine evaporated milk and margarine in saucepan. Bring to the boiling point. Remove from heat. Add sugar; stir until completely dissolved. Cook, covered, over medium heat for 2 to 3 minutes or until steam washes sugar crystals from side of pan. Boil for 8 minutes, stirring constantly. Remove from heat. Add remaining ingredients. Beat until mixture is thickened and creamy. Pour into 2 buttered 9-inch square dishes. Let stand until firm. Cut into squares. Yield: 5 pounds.

Ethel Chance, Maryland

ONE-BOWL PEANUT BUTTER FUDGE

¾ c. peanut butter
1 c. ground peanuts
½ c. corn syrup
½ c. butter, softened
4 c. confectioners' sugar

Combine all ingredients in large bowl; knead until well mixed. Pat into buttered 8-inch square dish. Chill until firm. Cut into 1-inch squares. Yield: 2 pounds.

Patricia Taylor, Kentucky

ORANGE-CARAMEL FUDGE

1 lg. can evaporated milk
1/4 c. butter
4 c. sugar
1/3 to 1/2 c. finely chopped orange rind
1 c. chopped walnuts

Combine evaporated milk and butter in saucepan. Bring to the boiling point. Remove from heat. Add 3 cups sugar; stir until completely dissolved. Cook, covered, over medium heat for 2 to 3 minutes or until steam washes sugar crystals from side of pan. Cook, uncovered, to 234 to 240 degrees on candy thermometer, soft-ball stage; do not stir. Cool to lukewarm, 110 degrees; do not stir. Caramelize remaining 1 cup sugar in skillet. Remove from heat. Add cooked mixture, orange rind and walnuts. Beat until mixture thickens and loses its luster. Pour into buttered 8-inch square dish. Let stand until firm. Cut into squares. Yield: 3 pounds.

Tissa Josten, Louisiana

NO-COOK PEANUTTY FUDGE

3/4 c. peanut butter
1/2 c. butter, softened
1/2 c. light corn syrup
1 tsp. vanilla extract
1/2 c. cocoa
3 1/2 c. sifted confectioners' sugar
1/2 c. chopped peanuts

Blend first 4 ingredients in bowl. Add cocoa and half the confectioners' sugar; mix well. Stir in remaining confectioners' sugar. Knead until smooth. Knead in peanuts. Press into buttered 8x8-inch dish. Let stand until set. Cut into squares. Yield: 2 1/2 pounds.

Lynda Wallar, Georgia

PEANUT-TOPPED FUDGE

1 c. evaporated milk
1/4 c. butter
2 1/2 c. sugar
1/4 tsp. salt
2 c. miniature marshmallows
1 tsp. vanilla extract
1/2 c. chunky peanut butter
2 c. milk chocolate chips

Combine evaporated milk and butter in saucepan. Bring to the boiling point. Remove from heat. Add sugar and salt; stir until completely dissolved. Cook, covered, over medium heat for 2 to 3 minutes or until steam washes sugar crystals from side of pan. Cook, uncovered, to 234 to 240 degrees on candy thermometer, soft-ball stage. Add marshmallows and vanilla; mix well. Combine peanut butter and 2 cups hot mixture in bowl; mix well. Add chocolate chips to remaining hot mixture. Stir until chocolate melts. Pour chocolate candy into foil-lined 9-inch square dish. Spread peanut butter candy over top. Chill for 1 hour or until firm. Cut into squares. Yield: 3 pounds.

Deanna Moore, Illinois

CRUNCHY PEANUT BUTTER FUDGE

1 c. milk
3 c. sugar
1/4 tsp. salt
3 1-oz. squares chocolate, grated
2 tbsp. light corn syrup
1 tsp. vanilla extract
1/4 c. peanut butter
1/4 c. butter
2/3 c. coarsely chopped salted peanuts

Bring milk to the boiling point in saucepan. Remove from heat. Stir in sugar, salt, chocolate and corn syrup. Stir until sugar is completely dissolved. Cook, covered, over medium heat for 2 to 3 minutes or until steam washes sugar crystals from side of pan. Cook, uncovered, to 234 to 240 degrees on candy thermometer, soft-ball stage; do not stir. Cool to 130 degrees; do not stir. Add vanilla, peanut butter and butter. Beat until mixture is thickened and loses its luster. Stir in peanuts. Pour into buttered 8-inch square dish. Let stand until firm. Cut into squares. Yield: 3 pounds.

Alice Miller, California

FESTIVE PEANUT BUTTER FUDGE

3/4 c. evaporated milk
1/4 c. margarine
2 1/4 c. sugar
1 7-oz. jar marshmallow creme
1 tsp. vanilla extract
1 12-oz. package peanut butter chips
1 c. broken pecans
1/4 c. chopped red candied cherries

Combine evaporated milk, margarine, sugar and marshmallow creme in 3-quart saucepan; mix well. Bring to a boil. Cook for 5 minutes, stirring constantly. Remove from heat. Add remaining ingredients; stir until peanut butter chips are completely melted. Pour into buttered 8x8-inch dish. Garnish with additional pecans and cherries. Let stand until set. Cut into squares. Yield: 3 pounds.

Janine Dorsey, Oklahoma

RICH CHOCOLATE FUDGE

3 c. sugar
1 env. unflavored gelatin
1 c. milk
½ c. light corn syrup
3 sq. unsweetened chocolate, grated
1½ c. butter
2 tsp. vanilla extract
1 c. chopped pecans

Combine sugar and gelatin in saucepan. Add milk, corn syrup, chocolate and butter. Cook over low heat until sugar dissolves completely, stirring constantly. Cook, covered, over medium heat for 2 to 3 minutes or until steam washes sugar crystals from side of pan. Cook, uncovered, to 234 to 240 degrees on candy thermometer, soft-ball stage; do not stir. Cool to lukewarm, 110 degrees; do not stir. Add vanilla. Beat until mixture thickens and loses its luster. Stir in pecans. Pour into buttered 9-inch square dish. Let stand until firm. Cut into squares. Yield: 3 pounds.

Betty Crickard, West Virginia

PERSIMMON FUDGE

2½ c. milk
6 c. sugar
¼ c. light corn syrup
1 c. pureed persimmon pulp
½ c. margarine
1 c. (or more) chopped nuts

Bring milk to the boiling point in saucepan. Remove from heat. Stir in sugar and corn syrup until sugar is completely dissolved. Add persimmon pulp; mix well. Cook, covered, over medium heat for 2 to 3 minutes or until steam washes sugar crystals from side of pan. Cook, uncovered, to 234 to 240 degrees on candy thermometer, soft-ball stage; do not stir. Cool to lukewarm, 110 degrees; do not stir. Add margarine. Beat until mixture is thickened and loses its luster. Stir in nuts. Pour into buttered 9x13-inch dish. Let stand until firm. Cut into squares. Yield: 2 pounds.

Pauline Roberts, California

PEPPERMINT FUDGE

3 c. sugar
¾ c. margarine, melted
⅔ c. evaporated milk
1 12-oz. package semisweet chocolate chips
1 7-oz. jar marshmallow creme
½ c. crushed peppermint candy
1 tsp. vanilla extract

Mix sugar, margarine and evaporated milk in 3-quart saucepan. Bring to a boil, stirring constantly. Boil for 5 minutes, stirring constantly; remove from heat. Stir in chocolate chips until melted. Beat in marshmallow creme, peppermint candy and vanilla. Pour into buttered 9x13-inch dish. Let stand until firm. Cut into squares. Yield: 3 pounds.

Linda Todd, Michigan

SOUR CREAM FUDGE

3 c. sugar
1 c. sour cream
⅛ tsp. soda
¼ c. dark corn syrup
6 tbsp. cocoa
⅛ tsp. salt
1 tsp. vanilla extract
1 c. chopped nuts

Combine sugar, sour cream, soda, corn syrup, cocoa and salt in saucepan. Cook over low heat until sugar dissolves completely, stirring constantly. Cook, covered, over medium heat for 2 to 3 minutes or until steam washes sugar crystals from side of pan. Cook, uncovered, to 234 to 240 degrees on candy thermometer, stirring occasionally only if necessary. Cool to lukewarm, 110 degrees; do not stir. Add vanilla. Beat until mixture thickens and loses its luster. Stir in nuts. Pour into buttered dish. Let stand until firm. Cut into squares. Yield: 3 pounds.

Allene Makenna, North Carolina

VELVEETA FUDGE

1 c. butter
8 oz. Velveeta cheese
1½ tsp. vanilla extract
2 lb. confectioners' sugar
½ c. cocoa
Chopped pecans (opt.)

Melt butter and cheese in saucepan over low heat, stirring constantly. Mix in vanilla. Pour over mixture of confectioners' sugar and cocoa in bowl; mix quickly until well blended. Spread in buttered 9x13-inch dish. Pat pecans over top. Let stand until set. Cut into squares. Yield: 3 pounds.

Erma Lee Sellers, Mississippi

◆◆◆◆◆◆◆◆◆◆◆◆◆◆◆◆◆◆◆◆◆◆◆◆◆◆◆◆◆◆

Hint: *To correct fudge that won't set up, combine with 1 or 2 teaspoons water and cook to specified temperature, stirring constantly.*

◆◆◆◆◆◆◆◆◆◆◆◆◆◆◆◆◆◆◆◆◆◆◆◆◆◆◆◆◆◆

FUDGE-RAISIN NUGGETS

1½ c. sugar
⅓ c. cocoa
¼ tsp. salt
¼ c. light corn syrup
½ c. milk
⅓ c. peanut butter
3 env. instant oatmeal with
   raisins and spice
1 c. salted peanuts

Combine first 5 ingredients in saucepan; mix well. Cook over medium heat until sugar dissolves completely, stirring constantly. Cook, covered, for 2 to 3 minutes or until steam washes sugar crystals from side of pan. Cook, uncovered, to 234 to 240 degrees on candy thermometer, soft-ball stage; do not stir. Remove from heat. Add peanut butter, oats and peanuts; mix well. Drop by teaspoonfuls onto waxed paper. Cool. Yield: 3 dozen.

Sharon Whitehurst, Tennessee

MARZIPAN

1 egg white
1 c. almond paste
1½ c. (about) confectioners' sugar
Lemon juice (opt.)
Paste or liquid food coloring

Beat egg white until frothy. Add almond paste gradually. Add enough confectioners' sugar gradually to make paste easy to handle. Add lemon juice 1 drop at a time if necessary to make of desired consistency. Shape into any fruit or other shapes as desired. Knead in paste food coloring or paint with diluted liquid food coloring if desired. Glaze paste candies with solution of gum arabic.
Strawberries—Tint, shape and texturize on small grater. Add cloves and angelica for stems.
Bananas—Tint, shape, and paint markings with brown food coloring.
Oranges—Proceed as for strawberries.
Apples and Pears—Tint, shape and paint blossom end brown. Add blush and cloves for stems.
Grapes—Tint, shape and arrange in cluster.

Catherine Will, Tennessee

CITRUS CANDIED PECANS

⅔ c. orange juice concentrate
3 c. sugar
3 c. pecan halves

Bring orange juice and sugar to a boil in heavy saucepan over medium heat. Cook to soft-ball stage or 240 degrees on candy thermometer. Fold in pecans. Spread on waxed paper. Cool. Break into pieces. Store in airtight container. Yield: 3 cups.

Earleen F. Williams, Florida

MEXICAN CANDY

2½ c. sugar
¼ tsp. salt
1 c. hot milk
1½ c. pecans
1 tsp. vanilla extract

Caramelize sugar and salt in heavy skillet, stirring constantly. Stir in milk gradually. Cook over medium heat to 234 to 240 degrees on candy thermometer, soft-ball stage, stirring constantly. Stir in pecans. Cook to 250 to 268 degrees, hard-ball stage, stirring constantly; remove from heat. Add vanilla. Beat until creamy. Drop by spoonfuls onto waxed paper. Yield: 2 pounds.

Daphne Smith, Texas

CHOCOLATE DINNER MINTS

1 lg. can evaporated milk
4 c. sugar
½ c. margarine
2 tsp. mint extract
1   12-oz. package chocolate chips
1   7-oz. jar marshmallow creme

Combine evaporated milk, sugar and margarine in saucepan. Cook over medium heat for 6 minutes, stirring constantly; remove from heat. Stir in remaining ingredients. Let stand until thickened. Drop by small teaspoonfuls onto waxed paper. Let stand until firm. Store in refrigerator or freezer. Yield: 4 pounds.

Bernadine Nelson, Montana

PARTY MINTS

2 c. sugar
1 stick butter
10 drops of desired flavoring
Food coloring (opt.)

Combine sugar, butter and 1 cup water in saucepan. Cook to 250 to 268 degrees on candy thermometer, hard-ball stage. Add flavoring and coloring; mix well. Pour onto marble slab; cool. Pull until smooth and firm. Divide into 4 long strips. Cut into small pieces with scissors. Store in cool place. Yield: 1 pound.

Connie Sword, Virginia

CINNAMON-COFFEE PECANS

2 tsp. instant coffee powder
¼ c. sugar
¼ tsp. cinnamon
Dash of salt
1½ c. pecan halves

Combine all ingredients and 2 tablespoons water in saucepan. Bring to a boil over medium heat. Boil for 3 minutes, stirring constantly. Spread on waxed paper. Separate pecans with 2 forks. Cool. Store in airtight container. Yield: 1½ cups.

Vivian Pierson, Illinois

CANDIED ORANGE SLICES

6 oranges
1½ c. packed dark brown sugar
Sugar

Place whole oranges in saucepan with water to cover. Simmer, covered, for 40 minutes or until rind is tender. Drain and cool. Cut each orange in half lengthwise; slice crosswise ⅜ inch thick. Layer orange slices in bowl. Mix brown sugar and 2 cups water in saucepan. Boil for 20 minutes or until thick and syrupy. Pour over orange slices. Refrigerate, covered, overnight. Drain. Coat each slice with sugar; place on wire rack. Let stand overnight or until dry. Coat each slice with sugar; pack into airtight container. Yield: 3 pounds.

Lillian Roden, Iowa

APRICOT PENUCHE

1½ c. sugar
1 c. packed light brown sugar
⅓ c. light cream
⅓ c. milk
2 tbsp. butter
1 tsp. vanilla extract
½ c. finely chopped, dried
   California apricots
⅓ c. finely chopped pecans

Combine first 5 ingredients in 2-quart saucepan; mix well. Bring to a boil over medium heat, stirring constantly. Cook, covered, for 2 to 3 minutes or until steam washes sugar crystals from side of pan. Cook, uncovered, to 238 degrees on candy thermometer, soft-ball stage; do not stir. Cool to lukewarm, 110 degrees; do not stir. Add vanilla; beat until mixture thickens and loses its luster. Stir in apricots and pecans. Spread in buttered 8-inch square dish. Score warm candy into squares. Garnish each with additional apricot piece. Cool. Cut into squares. Yield: 1½ pounds.

Photograph for this recipe on page 58.

ORANGE DROPS

3 c. sugar
1½ c. milk, scalded
Pinch of salt
¼ c. butter
Grated rind of 2 oranges
1 c. chopped pecans

Caramelize 1 cup sugar in large saucepan. Add milk all at once; mix well. Bring to the boiling point; remove from heat. Add remaining 2 cups sugar and salt; mix until completely dissolved. Cook, covered, for 2 to 3 minutes or until steam washes sugar crystals from side of pan. Cook, uncovered, to 240 to 248 degrees on candy thermometer, soft-ball stage; do not stir. Cool to lukewarm, 110 degrees. Add remaining ingredients. Beat until creamy. Drop by spoonfuls onto waxed paper. Let stand until firm. Yield: 2 pounds.

Marilyn Becker, Kansas

MICROWAVE QUICK PENUCHE

1   7-oz. jar marshmallow creme
1 sm. can evaporated milk
6 tbsp. margarine
1¾ c. sugar
¼ tsp. salt
1   6-oz. package butterscotch chips
1 c. chopped walnuts

Combine first 5 ingredients in large glass bowl. Microwave on High for 6 minutes or until mixture comes to the boiling point, stirring twice. Microwave on Medium for 3 minutes, stirring once. Add butterscotch chips; stir until melted. Stir in walnuts. Spoon into buttered, foil-lined 8-inch square dish. Chill until firm. Cut into squares. Yield: 2 pounds.

Judy Adler, Texas

QUICK PENUCHE FUDGE

½ c. melted margarine
1 c. packed brown sugar
¼ c. milk
1⅔ to 2 c. confectioners' sugar

Combine margarine and brown sugar in saucepan. Cook until sugar dissolves, stirring constantly. Add milk; blend well. Cook for 1 minute, stirring constantly. Remove from heat. Cool. Stir in enough confectioners' sugar gradually to make of desired consistency. Pour into buttered 8x8-inch dish. Chill until firm. Cut into squares. Yield: 1 pound.

Diane Norbury, Michigan

BUTTERMILK PRALINES

1 c. buttermilk
3 c. sugar
1 tsp. soda
⅛ tsp. salt
¾ c. dark corn syrup
2 tbsp. butter, softened
2 c. nuts

Heat buttermilk to the boiling point in saucepan. Remove from heat. Add sugar, soda, salt, corn syrup and butter. Stir until sugar is completely dissolved. Cook, covered, over medium heat for 2 to 3 minutes or until steam washes sugar crystals from side of pan. Cook, uncovered, to 234 to 240 degrees on candy thermometer, soft-ball stage; do not stir. Cool to lukewarm, 110 degrees; do not stir. Add nuts. Beat until mixture is thickened and loses its luster. Drop by spoonfuls onto waxed paper. Let stand until firm. Store in airtight container. Yield: 3½ pounds.

Patricia Stupka, Texas

BUTTERY PECAN PRALINES

2 c. sugar
1 tsp. soda
1 c. buttermilk
⅛ tsp. salt
2 tbsp. butter
2½ c. pecan halves

Combine sugar, soda, buttermilk and salt in saucepan. Cook over high heat for 5 minutes or to 210 degrees on candy thermometer, stirring frequently. Add butter and pecans. Cook to 234 to 240 degrees on candy thermometer, soft-ball stage. Cool slightly. Beat until thick and creamy. Drop by tablespoonfuls onto waxed paper. Let stand until firm. Store in airtight container. Yield: 2 pounds.

Sunday Belcher, Texas

ORANGE PRALINES

1 c. cream
3 c. sugar
2 tbsp. light corn syrup
Finely chopped rind of 1 orange
2 c. pecans

Bring cream to the boiling point in saucepan. Remove from heat. Add sugar and corn syrup; stir until sugar is completely dissolved. Cook, covered, over medium heat for 2 to 3 minutes or until steam washes sugar crystals from side of pan. Cook, uncovered, to 234 to 240 degrees on candy thermometer, soft-ball stage; do not stir. Add orange rind and pecans; mix well.

Drop by spoonfuls onto waxed paper. Let stand until firm. Store in airtight container. Yield: 2½ pounds.

Martha Bailey, Tennessee

CHEWY PRALINES

1 sm. can evaporated milk
2 c. light corn syrup
¾ c. sugar
1 can sweetened condensed milk
¼ c. margarine
1 tsp. salt
3 c. broken pecans

Bring evaporated milk to the boiling point in saucepan. Remove from heat. Stir in corn syrup and sugar; stir until sugar is completely dissolved. Cook, covered, over medium heat for 2 to 3 minutes or until steam washes sugar crystals from side of pan. Cook, uncovered, over medium heat to 240 to 248 degrees on candy thermometer, firm-ball stage; do not stir. Add condensed milk and margarine. Cook to 234 to 240 degrees, soft-ball stage, stirring constantly. Remove from heat. Stir in salt and pecans. Drop by tablespoonfuls onto foil. Let stand until firm. Wrap individually in plastic wrap. Yield: 4 pounds.

Robin Weynand, Texas

TEXAS PRALINES

¾ c. milk
2 c. sugar
½ tsp. soda
1½ c. pecan halves
1 tsp. vanilla extract
1 tbsp. butter
¼ tsp. salt

Bring milk to the boiling point in saucepan. Remove from heat. Add sugar and soda; stir until sugar is completely dissolved. Cook, covered, over medium heat for 2 to 3 minutes or until steam washes sugar crystals from side of pan. Cook, uncovered, to 234 to 240 degrees on candy thermometer, soft-ball stage; do not stir. Cool to lukewarm, 110 degrees; do not stir. Add remaining ingredients. Beat until mixture is thickened and loses its luster. Drop by tablespoonfuls onto waxed paper sprinkled with salt. Let stand until firm. Store in airtight container. Yield: 2 pounds.

Mary Mouser, Texas

◆◆◆◆◆◆◆◆◆◆◆◆◆◆◆◆◆◆◆◆◆◆◆◆◆◆◆◆◆

Hint: *To prevent crystallization, use only clean, dry thermometers, spoons and utensils for candy making.*

◆◆◆◆◆◆◆◆◆◆◆◆◆◆◆◆◆◆◆◆◆◆◆◆◆◆◆◆◆

OLD-FASHIONED ROCK CANDY

   3 c. fruit juice
   6 c. sugar
   ¾ tsp. cream of tartar
   Food coloring (opt.)
   Flavoring (opt.)

Bring fruit juice to the boiling point in saucepan. Remove from heat. Add remaining ingredients; stir until sugar dissolves completely. Cook, covered, over high heat for 2 to 3 minutes or until steam washes sugar crystals from side of pan. Cook, uncovered, to 270 to 290 degrees on candy thermometer, soft-crack stage; do not stir. Pour into buttered dish. Chill until firm. Break into pieces. Store in airtight container. Yield: 2 pounds.
Note: For basic rock candy, substitute 3 cups water for fruit juice.

Kathy Huset, California

SOUR CREAM DELIGHTS

   1 c. packed light brown sugar
   ½ c. sugar
   ½ c. sour cream
   Pinch of salt
   2 c. walnut halves

Combine sugars, sour cream and salt in saucepan. Cook over low heat until sugars are completely dissolved, stirring constantly. Cook to 234 to 240 degrees on candy thermometer, soft-ball stage; do not stir. Remove from heat. Add walnuts; mix well. Spread on waxed paper-lined surface. Separate walnuts with 2 forks. Let stand until firm. Store in airtight container. Yield: 1½ pounds.

Lorraine Mason, California

SEAFOAM CANDY

   ½ c. light corn syrup
   2 c. packed light brown sugar
   ¼ tsp. salt
   2 egg whites, stiffly beaten
   1 tsp. vanilla extract
   1 c. chopped nuts

Bring ½ cup water to the boiling point in saucepan. Remove from heat. Add corn syrup, brown sugar and salt; stir until completely dissolved. Cook, covered, for 2 to 3 minutes or until steam washes sugar crystals from side of pan. Cook, uncovered, to 250 to 268 degrees on candy thermometer, hard-ball stage; do not stir. Pour over stiffly beaten egg whites, beating constantly until stiff peaks form; do not scrape pan. Stir in vanilla and nuts. Drop by small spoonfuls onto waxed paper. Let stand until firm. Yield: 1½ pounds.

Hilda Swenson, Arkansas

WALNUT SEAFOAM

   3 c. packed light brown sugar
   1 tbsp. light corn syrup
   2 egg whites, stiffly beaten
   2 tsp. vanilla extract
   1 c. chopped walnuts

Combine brown sugar, corn syrup and ¾ cup water in heavy saucepan. Bring to a boil, stirring constantly. Cook, covered, for 2 to 3 minutes or until steam washes sugar crystals from side of pan. Cook, uncovered, to 240 degrees on candy thermometer, firm-ball stage. Remove ⅔ cup syrup. Pour over stiffly beaten egg whites, beating constantly. Cook remaining syrup to 256 degrees, hard-ball stage. Add to egg white mixture gradually, beating constantly. Add vanilla. Beat until mixture loses its luster. Stir in walnuts. Drop by spoonfuls onto lightly buttered surface. Let stand until firm.

Photograph for this recipe on this page.

OLD-FASHIONED SPONGE CANDY

1 c. sugar
1 c. dark corn syrup
1 tbsp. vinegar
1 tbsp. soda, sifted

Mix sugar, corn syrup and vinegar in saucepan. Cook to 300 to 310 degrees on candy thermometer, hard-crack stage, stirring constantly. Remove from heat. Stir in soda. Pour into buttered 9-inch square dish. Do not scrape bottom or side of pan. Cool on wire rack. Break into pieces. Store in airtight container. Yield: 1 pound.

Audrey Taylor, Rhode Island

SALT WATER TAFFY

1 c. light corn syrup
2 c. sugar
1½ tsp. salt
2 tbsp. butter
¼ tsp. oil of peppermint
7 drops of green food coloring

Bring corn syrup and 1 cup water to a boil in saucepan. Remove from heat. Stir in sugar and salt until completely dissolved. Cook, covered, over medium heat for 2 to 3 minutes or until steam washes sugar crystals from side of pan. Cook, uncovered, to 250 to 268 degrees on candy thermometer, hard-ball stage; do not stir. Remove from heat. Add remaining ingredients; do not stir. Pour into buttered 12x15-inch dish. Let stand until cool enough to handle. Mix with spatula to blend ingredients. Pull with buttered hands until light colored and stiff. Cut into 4 portions. Pull each into ½-inch thick strand. Cut into bite-sized pieces with buttered scissors. Yield: 1½ pounds.

Juli Royalty, Oklahoma

ENGLISH TOFFEE

2 sticks butter
1 c. sugar
1 tsp. light corn syrup
1 c. finely chopped almonds
Salt to taste
⅛ tsp. soda
16 oz. milk chocolate, melted
1 c. chopped walnuts

Combine butter, sugar, corn syrup, almonds and salt in saucepan. Cook over low heat until sugar is completely dissolved, stirring constantly. Cook over medium heat to 300 to 310 degrees on candy thermometer, hard-crack stage; do not stir. Remove from heat. Stir in soda. Spread half the melted chocolate over bottom of 9x13-inch dish lined with buttered foil. Pour toffee into prepared dish. Let stand until firm. Spread remaining chocolate over top. Sprinkle with walnuts. Let stand until set. Break into pieces. Yield: 2½ pounds.

Marty Woodward, Colorado

MICROWAVE ALMOND TOFFEE

¾ c. butter
1 c. packed brown sugar
¾ c. finely chopped almonds
½ c. semisweet chocolate chips, melted

Microwave butter and brown sugar in glass bowl on High for 1 minute. Beat until smooth. Microwave for 4 minutes. Stir in ½ cup almonds. Microwave for 2 minutes or until thick. Beat with wire whisk. Pour into 8x8-inch dish lined with buttered foil. Sprinkle chocolate chips over top. Let stand, covered with plastic wrap, for 4 minutes. Spread melted chocolate over top. Sprinkle with ¼ cup almonds. Chill until chocolate is firm. Peel off foil. Break into pieces. Store in airtight container in refrigerator. Yield: 1 pound.

Vonita Tast, California

◆◆◆◆◆◆◆◆◆◆◆◆◆◆◆◆◆◆◆◆◆◆◆◆◆◆◆◆◆

Hint: *Never add water to melted chocolate chips. The result is an unusable grainy mass.*

◆◆◆◆◆◆◆◆◆◆◆◆◆◆◆◆◆◆◆◆◆◆◆◆◆◆◆◆◆

ALMOND ROCA

½ c. butter
½ c. margarine
1⅓ c. sugar
1 c. sliced almonds
1 8-oz. milk chocolate bar, broken
1 c. ground walnuts

Melt butter and margarine in heavy iron skillet. Stir in sugar. Cook until mixture is lemon-colored and bubbly, stirring constantly with wooden spoon. Add sliced almonds. Cook until mixture is lightly browned, stirring constantly. Pour onto foil-lined baking sheet. Sprinkle with half the chocolate. Let stand until chocolate melts. Spread over almond mixture. Top with half the walnuts. Invert on foil. Top with remaining chocolate; spread. Sprinkle with remaining walnuts. Yield: 2 pounds.

Polly Hanst, West Virginia

TOFFEE

½ c. butter
½ c. margarine
1 c. sugar
1 tbsp. light corn syrup
1 c. chopped nuts
1   12-oz. package chocolate chips
2 tbsp. melted paraffin

Melt butter and margarine in heavy 3-quart saucepan over medium heat. Add sugar, 3 tablespoons water and corn syrup. Cook, covered, over medium heat for 2 to 3 minutes or until steam washes sugar crystals from side of pan. Cook, uncovered, to 270 to 290 degrees on candy thermometer, soft-crack stage; do not stir. Add nuts. Cook for 3 minutes longer. Pour into buttered 10x15-inch dish. Spread into thin layer. Let stand until firm. Place on waxed paper; blot with paper towel. Melt chocolate chips in double boiler. Blend in paraffin. Spread chocolate over toffee. Let stand until firm. Break into pieces. Yield: 2 pounds.

Mary Louise Hedrick, West Virginia

◆◆◆◆◆◆◆◆◆◆◆◆◆◆◆◆◆◆◆◆◆◆◆◆◆◆◆◆

Hint: *To prevent overcooking, remove pan from heat when testing candy by the cold water tests.*

◆◆◆◆◆◆◆◆◆◆◆◆◆◆◆◆◆◆◆◆◆◆◆◆◆◆◆◆

CHOCOLATE-ALMOND TOFFEE

1 c. packed brown sugar
1 c. sugar
⅓ c. light corn syrup
⅛ tsp. salt
⅓ c. butter
1   6-oz. package semisweet chocolate
     chips, melted
½ c. toasted almonds, chopped

Bring ½ cup water to the boiling point in saucepan. Remove from heat. Add sugars, corn syrup and salt. Stir until sugars are completely dissolved. Cook, covered, over high heat for 2 to 3 minutes or until steam washes sugar crystals from side of pan. Cook, uncovered, to 240 to 248 degrees on candy thermometer, firm-ball stage; do not stir. Add butter. Cook to 300 to 310 degrees on candy thermometer, hard-crack stage; do not stir. Pour into lightly oiled 9x9-inch dish. Cool until brittle. Spread with half the melted chocolate. Sprinkle with half the almonds. Let stand until chocolate is set. Invert on waxed paper-lined surface. Spread with remaining chocolate; sprinkle with remaining almonds. Let stand until set. Break into pieces. Yield: 2 pounds.

Katie Johnson, Georgia

WALNUT TOFFEE

1½ c. butter, melted
2 c. sugar
1 tsp. salt
1 tbsp. light corn syrup
1½ c. coarsely chopped Diamond walnuts
4 oz. chocolate, chopped
½ c. finely chopped walnuts

Combine butter, sugar, salt, corn syrup and ½ cup water in heavy saucepan. Bring to a boil, stirring constantly. Cook, covered, for 2 to 3 minutes or until steam washes sugar crystals from side of pan. Cook, uncovered, to 290 degrees on candy thermometer, soft-crack stage; do not stir. Remove from heat. Stir in coarsely chopped walnuts. Pour into buttered 10x15-inch pan. Cool for 10 minutes or until candy feels warm to the touch, sprinkle with chocolate. Let stand until melted; spread with spatula. Sprinkle finely chopped walnuts over top. Let stand until firm. Break into pieces. Yield: 2 pounds.

Photograph for this recipe on page 75.

◆◆◆◆◆◆◆◆◆◆◆◆◆◆◆◆◆◆◆◆◆◆◆◆◆◆◆◆

Hint: *To use leftover melted chocolate, coat cookies, marshmallows, or graham crackers. Or stir in cereal, nuts, raisins and drop by spoonfuls onto waxed paper to cool.*

◆◆◆◆◆◆◆◆◆◆◆◆◆◆◆◆◆◆◆◆◆◆◆◆◆◆◆◆

TURTLES

2 c. sugar
2 c. light corn syrup
1 stick butter
2 c. whipping cream
½ can sweetened condensed milk
16 oz. pecan halves
1 lb. dipping chocolate, melted

Combine sugar and corn syrup in covered saucepan. Bring to a boil. Cook for 2 minutes. Add butter. Stir until butter melts. Combine cream and condensed milk in double boiler. Cook over hot water until heated through. Do not boil. Add to corn syrup mixture 2 tablespoons at a time, mixing well after each addition. Cook to 230 to 240 degrees on candy thermometer, soft-ball stage. Arrange pecan halves in pairs on buttered platter. Spoon 1 tablespoon candy mixture over each pair. Let stand until firm. Coat with chocolate. Place in paper bonbon cups. Yield: 5 pounds.

Pat Rosenbaum, Montana

Confections Know-How

Confections — fun to make and fun to eat — are the novice cook's specialty. Easy success with *no cooking* is a guaranteed confidence-builder. In no time at all, you will be serving elaborate creations with ease.

When you find yourself rushed for time, but really want something impressive for company, look over the recipes in this section for no-cook confections that will turn heads! Chocolate-Peanut Clusters, Easy Pecan Roll and Angel Cookies arranged on a tray will be the center of attention at any gathering!

Many of these recipes can be prepared in a matter of minutes with staple items from your pantry. Since melting butter and chocolate are the only cooking procedures usually required, confections are perfect treats for any day! For maximum ease in serving, keep your confections dainty — small, pretty, bite-sized goodies.

This section is a treasure-trove for children. There are many recipes that even small children enjoy "cooking" — Bunny Tails, Putterfingers and even Homemade Tootsie Rolls! Imagine how proud they'll be to serve these homemady-by-them treats to their friends!

Confections are family favorites any time. And, there's an added bonus — they travel well! Wrapped and packed between layers of crumpled waxed paper, these tasty tidbits are delightful gifts to send down the street or across the country. Mail several tins of assorted confections for special occasions or just to make someone's day a little more special!

Confections to Make with Fondant

One of the most versatile candy basics is fondant, both cooked and uncooked (see page 66 for basic recipes). A batch may be stored, tightly covered, for several weeks, then flavored, tinted and shaped to suit your fancy!

Vanilla French Creams: Flavor 2 cups fondant with 1 teaspoon vanilla. Shape into ¾-inch balls. Dip in melted dipping chocolate; roll in crushed nuts. Let stand until firm.

Chocolate French Creams: Add 1 ounce melted chocolate to 2 cups fondant. Shape into ¾-inch balls. Dip in melted dipping chocolate; roll in chocolate sprinkles. Let stand until firm.

Fondant Cut-outs: Roll fondant to 1-inch thickness on surface sprinkled with mixture of cornstarch and confectioners' sugar. Cut with small shaped cookie cutters. Let stand until firm.

Stuffed Fruits: Shape fondant into small balls. Stuff into pitted dates, prunes or dried apricots. Roll in sugar. Let stand until firm.

Frosted Fruits and Nuts: Dip walnut or pecan halves, whole blanched almonds, candied cherries, pitted dates or dried apricots into melted fondant. Let stand until firm.

Nut Bonbons: Sandwich walnut or pecan halves together with small amounts of fondant. Let stand until firm.

Thin Mints: Flavor fondant with peppermint and tint green or flavor with wintergreen and tint pale pink. Melt in double boiler. Drop by teaspoonfuls onto waxed paper. Let stand until firm.

Peanut Butter Pinwheels: Roll fondant into rectangle. Spread with peanut butter. Roll as for jelly roll. Cut into slices. Let stand until firm.

Peppermint Patties: Flavor 2 cups fondant with ¼ teaspoon oil of peppermint. Tint with green food coloring. Shape into 1-inch balls; flatten into patties. Dip in semisweet dipping chocolate. Let stand until firm.

Snowballs: Shape fondant into small balls. Roll in flaked coconut. Let stand until firm.

Sugarplums: Roll fondant around candied cherries, preserved ginger or pieces of dried apricots. Let stand until firm.

Violet Creams: Knead 4 drops of purple food coloring and ¼ teaspoon violet extgract into 1 pound fondant. Shape into walnut-sized balls. Flatten slightly. Press crystallized violet into each cream. Let stand for 1 hour.

Crystallized Violets: Combine ½ ounce gum arabic and 1 tablespoon rose water in jar. Shake for 3 minutes. Let stand for 3 hours or until gum arabic dissolves, shaking occasionally. Cut stalks from violets, leaving ¼-inch stem. Paint both sides with gum arabic. Dip in sugar. Let stand on waxed paper for 24 hours or until dry.

ANGEL COOKIES

1 c. sugar
½ c. melted butter
1 8-oz. package dates, chopped
2 c. crispy rice cereal
1 c. coconut
Confectioners' sugar

Combine sugar, butter, and dates in saucepan. Cook over low heat until thick, stirring constantly. Cool. Add cereal and coconut; mix well. Shape into walnut-sized balls. Roll in confectioners' sugar. Place in paper bonbon cups. Store in airtight container. Yield: 2½ pounds.

Aileen Hurley, Illinois

APRICOT BALLS

1 8-oz. package dried apricots, finely chopped
2½ c. flaked coconut
¾ c. sweetened condensed milk
⅔ c. chopped pecans
Pecan meal

Combine apricots, coconut, condensed milk and pecans in bowl; mix well. Shape into 1-inch balls. Roll in pecan meal; place in paper bonbon cups. Let stand for 2 hours or until firm. Yield: 4 dozen.

Margaret Hunter, Indiana

MICROWAVE APRICOT CHEWIES

1 c. butter
1⅓ c. packed dark brown sugar
⅔ c. honey
3 c. quick-cooking oats
2 c. finely chopped dried apricots
1 c. shredded coconut
1 c. chopped almonds
1 c. wheat germ

Microwave butter in 2-quart glass baking dish on High for 1 minute or until melted. Blend in brown sugar and honey. Add remaining ingredients; mix well. Spread evenly in dish. Microwave on High for 6 minutes or until firm but moist, stirring once. Cool slightly. Shape into bite-sized balls; place in paper bonbon cups. Store in airtight container. Yield: 8 dozen.

Donae Parker, Texas

BUNNY TAILS

1 6-oz. can frozen orange juice concentrate, thawed

1 12-oz. box vanilla wafers, crushed
1 16-oz. package confectioners' sugar
1 c. chopped pecans
1 stick margarine, melted
Flaked coconut

Combine all ingredients except coconut in bowl; mix well. Shape into small balls; roll in coconut. Place in paper bonbon cups. Store in airtight container in refrigerator. Yield: 2½ pounds.

Phyllis Weber, Minnesota

BUTTERSCOTCH-WALNUT LOG

1 6-oz. package butterscotch chips
⅓ c. sweetened condensed milk
½ tsp. vanilla extract
⅔ c. coarsely chopped walnuts
1 egg white, beaten

Melt butterscotch chips in double boiler; remove from heat. Blend in condensed milk and vanilla. Stir in half the walnuts. Chill until firm. Shape into 12-inch log. Score with fork. Brush with egg white. Roll in remaining walnuts. Chill, wrapped, until firm. Cut into ½-inch slices. Yield: 1 pound.

Becky Leonard, California

BOURBON BALLS

1 6-oz. package semisweet chocolate chips, melted
½ c. sugar
⅓ c. Bourbon
2½ c. fine vanilla wafer crumbs
½ c. finely chopped walnuts
Confectioners' sugar

Mix chocolate and sugar in bowl until smooth. Blend in Bourbon. Add mixture of crumbs and walnuts; mix well. Shape into 1-inch balls. Roll in confectioners' sugar; place in paper bonbon cups. Store in airtight container for several days. Sprinkle with additional Bourbon if desired. Yield: 1½ dozen.

Gladys Koller, Utah

CHOCOLATE-COVERED GINGER

3 oz. semisweet chocolate
3 3-oz. packages candied ginger.

Melt chocolate in double boiler over hot water. Dip ends of ginger in chocolate to coat. Place on wire rack. Let stand until firm. Store between layers of waxed paper in airtight container.

Photograph for this recipe on page 54.

CREAMY CHOCOLATE SQUARES

1 16-oz. package confectioners' sugar
2 3-oz. packages cream cheese, softened
4 sq. semisweet chocolate, melted
1 tbsp. vanilla extract
¾ c. chopped walnuts

Cream confectioners' sugar and cream cheese in bowl until light and fluffy. Blend in chocolate and vanilla. Add walnuts; mix well. Pour into buttered 8-inch dish. Chill until firm. Cut into squares.
Yield: 2 pounds.

Judith Hader, California

CHOCOLATE HONEY BEARS

1 6-oz. package semisweet chocolate chips
3 tbsp. honey
3 c. confectioners' sugar
1¼ c. chopped pecans
2½ tsp. instant coffee powder
1¾ c. fine vanilla wafer crumbs
1 8-oz. milk chocolate bar with nuts

Melt chocolate chips in double boiler over hot water. Stir in honey, confectioners' sugar, pecans, coffee, ⅓ cup hot water and crumbs. Mix well. Cut candy bar into small pieces. Shape a small amount of pecan mixture around each piece; place on waxed paper. Let stand until firm. Store in tightly closed container for 24 hours or longer before serving.

Sharon Ritchie, Colorado

COCONUT-FUDGE MELTAWAYS

½ c. butter
2½ sq. unsweetened chocolate
¼ c. sugar
2 tsp. vanilla extract
1 egg, beaten
2 c. graham cracker crumbs
1 c. coconut
½ c. chopped nuts
¼ c. melted butter
1 tbsp. milk
2 c. sifted confectioners' sugar

Melt ½ cup butter and 1 square chocolate in saucepan over low heat. Add sugar, 1 teaspoon vanilla and next 4 ingredients; mix well. Press into 9x9-inch pan. Chill until firm. Mix ¼ cup melted butter, milk, confectioners' sugar and 1 teaspoon vanilla in bowl. Spread over crumb mixture. Chill until firm. Melt remaining 1½ squares chocolate in saucepan over low heat. Spread over chilled filling. Chill until almost firm. Cut into tiny squares. Yield: 3½ dozen.

Renee Johnson, Washington

COCONUT JOYS

½ c. melted butter
2 c. confectioners' sugar
3 c. coconut
2 sq. dark chocolate, melted

Combine first 3 ingredients in bowl; mix well. Shape into balls; place in paper bonbon cups. Make indentation in center of each ball. Fill with chocolate. Chill until firm. Store in refrigerator. Yield: 3 dozen.

Tonia Bible, Texas

HAYSTACKS

1 3-oz. package cream cheese, softened
¼ c. milk
4 c. confectioners' sugar
4 oz. unsweetened chocolate, melted
½ tsp. vanilla extract
Dash of salt
6 c. miniature marshmallows
7 oz. flaked coconut

Blend cream cheese and milk in bowl. Mix in confectioners' sugar gradually. Stir in chocolate, vanilla and salt. Fold in marshmallows. Drop by heaping spoonfuls into coconut; toss to coat. Place on waxed paper-lined tray. Chill for 1 hour or until firm.

Drenda Bland, New Jersey

CHRISTMAS KISS KANDIES

¾ c. slivered almonds
½ c. confectioners' sugar
5 tsp. light corn syrup
1 tsp. almond extract
⅛ tsp. red food coloring
⅛ tsp. green food coloring
1 6-oz. package milk chocolate kisses
1 c. sugar

Process almonds in blender until very finely chopped. Combine with confectioners' sugar in bowl. Add mixture of corn syrup and flavoring gradually, stirring constantly until blended. Divide into 2 portions. Tint 1 portion red and 1 portion green. Shape by teaspoonfuls around chocolate kisses, maintaining kiss shape. Roll in sugar. Store in airtight container.

Photograph for this recipe on page 53.

◆◆◆◆◆◆◆◆◆◆◆◆◆◆◆◆◆◆◆◆◆◆◆◆◆◆◆

Hint: *To avoid white streaks on chocolate-coated candy, bring candy centers to room temperature before dipping them into chocolate.*

◆◆◆◆◆◆◆◆◆◆◆◆◆◆◆◆◆◆◆◆◆◆◆◆◆◆◆

KRIS KRINGLES

1   6-oz. package semisweet chocolate chips
2 tbsp. margarine
1 egg
1 c. sifted confectioners' sugar
½ tsp. vanilla extract
Dash of salt
½ c. flaked coconut
½ c. chopped dry-roasted peanuts

Melt chocolate chips and margarine in saucepan over low heat, stirring constantly. Cool to lukewarm. Beat in egg until smooth and glossy. Add confectioners' sugar, vanilla and salt; mix well. Stir in coconut and peanuts. Chill in refrigerator. Shape into 10-inch roll. Chill, wrapped, for several hours. Cut into ¼-inch slices. Yield: 3 dozen.

Doreen Kennedy, Connecticut

CHOCOLATY GRANOLA

2 c. oats
1 c. wheat germ
½ c. sesame seed
½ c. coconut
⅔ c. peanut butter
½ c. honey
2 tbsp. oil
1 tsp. vanilla extract
½ tsp. salt
1   6-oz. package chocolate chips, melted
1 c. confectioners' sugar

Combine first 4 ingredients in baking pan; mix well. Blend peanut butter, honey, oil, vanilla and salt in bowl. Pour over oats mixture; mix well. Bake at 300 degrees for 45 minutes. Stir to crumble. Blend chocolate and confectioners' sugar in bowl. Stir into granola. Shape as desired. Yield: 3 dozen.

Julie Baird, Texas

GORP BARS

1 c. corn syrup
½ c. packed brown sugar
¼ tsp. salt
1½ c. peanut butter
1 tsp. vanilla extract
1 c. nonfat dry milk powder
2 c. granola
1   6-oz. package chocolate chips

Combine corn syrup, brown sugar and salt in saucepan. Bring to a boil over high heat, stirring constantly. Stir in peanut butter; remove from heat. Add remaining ingredients; mix well. Pour into rectangular dish. Chill for 30 minutes. Cut into bars. Chill for 30 minutes longer. Yield: 3 pounds.

JoAnn Stanton, California

HEATH BARS

12 whole graham crackers
2 sticks margarine
1¼ c. packed brown sugar
1¼ c. chopped pecans
8 milk chocolate bars

Arrange single layer of graham crackers in greased 10x15-inch baking pan. Bring margarine, brown sugar and pecans to a boil in saucepan. Cook for 2 minutes, stirring constantly. Pour over graham crackers. Bake at 350 degrees for 9 minutes. Place chocolate bars on top. Let stand until chocolate melts. Spread evenly. Cool in freezer until set. Cut into bars. Yield: 4 dozen.

D'Ann Spinics, Texas

MILLIONAIRE CONFECTIONS

4½ c. sugar
1 tbsp. butter
1 lg. can evaporated milk
5 c. pecan halves
2   6-oz. packages semisweet chocolate chips
1   10-oz. jar marshmallow creme

Combine first 3 ingredients in saucepan. Bring to a boil, stirring constantly. Cook for 10 minutes, stirring constantly. Combine pecans, chocolate chips and marshmallow creme in bowl; mix well. Pour into cooked mixture; mix lightly. Drop by small spoonfuls onto waxed paper. Let stand until firm. Yield: 5½ pounds.

Robin Stroud, North Carolina

CHOCOLATE MINT CUPS

1 c. butter, softened
2 c. confectioners' sugar
4 sq. unsweetened chocolate, melted
4 eggs, beaten
1 tsp. peppermint extract
3 tbsp. vanilla wafer crumbs

Blend first 3 ingredients in bowl. Beat in eggs 1 at a time. Stir in flavoring. Sprinkle ¼ teaspoon crumbs into each of 36 paper-lined miniature muffin cups. Fill with chocolate mixture. Freeze until firm. Garnish each with whipped topping and cherry. Yield: 1½ pounds.

Marge Haggland, Alaska

PEPPERMINT CRUNCHIES

½ c. evaporated milk
½ c. sugar
1 tbsp. light corn syrup
1 6-oz. package semisweet chocolate chips
½ c. coarsely chopped peppermint
  stick candy
1 c. chopped nuts

Combine first 3 ingredients in saucepan. Bring to a boil, stirring constantly. Boil for 2 minutes, stirring constantly; remove from heat. Stir in chocolate chips until melted. Cool for 10 minutes. Stir in candy and nuts. Drop by teaspoonfuls onto waxed paper. Chill for several hours. Yield: 1 pound.

Elva Koenig, Iowa

NUT CLUSTER CUPS

1 6-oz. package milk or semisweet
  chocolate chips
1 tsp. shortening
1 c. broken nuts

Melt chocolate and shortening in double boiler over hot water. Stir in nuts. Drop by spoonfuls into 1-inch paper bonbon cups. Chill until firm. Yield: 1¼ dozen.

Photograph for this recipe on Cover.

CHOCOLATE OATMEAL DROPS

2 c. sugar
½ tsp. salt
¼ c. cocoa
¼ c. margarine
½ c. milk
2 c. quick-cooking oats
½ c. peanut butter
1 tsp. vanilla extract

Mix sugar, salt and cocoa in saucepan. Add margarine and milk. Bring to a boil. Cook for 1½ minutes. Add remaining ingredients; mix well. Drop by teaspoonfuls onto waxed paper; cool.

Marilake Farmer, Arkansas

O'HENRY BARS

1 c. sugar
1 c light corn syrup
1 c. peanut butter
5 c. Special K cereal
1 c. Spanish peanuts
Chocolate frosting

Combine sugar and corn syrup in large saucepan. Cook until sugar is dissolved, stirring constantly. Add peanut butter; mix well. Stir in cereal and peanuts. Press into 9x15-inch dish. Spread with frosting. Cut into bars. Yield: 2 dozen.

Kellie Dawson, Missouri

CHOCOLATE-PEANUT CLUSTERS

1 6-oz. package chocolate chips
⅔ c. sweetened condensed milk
1 tsp. vanilla extract
1½ c. salted Spanish peanuts

Melt chocolate chips in top of double boiler over hot water. Remove from heat. Add condensed milk, vanilla and peanuts; mix well. Drop by teaspoonfuls onto waxed paper. Cool. Yield: 1½ dozen.

Megan Martin, Illinois

MOCHA-PEANUT CLUSTERS

1 c. semisweet chocolate chips
16 lg. marshmallows, quartered
⅓ c. butter
1 tbsp. instant coffee powder
2 c. salted peanuts

Melt first 3 ingredients in double boiler, stirring occasionally. Add coffee powder. Remove from heat. Stir in peanuts. Drop by teaspoonfuls onto waxed paper. Cool. Yield: 1½ pounds.

Juanita Lunn, Ohio

PEANUT BUTTER LOGS

1 c. peanut butter
¼ c. margarine, softened
1½ c. sifted confectioners' sugar
3 c. Kellogg's Rice Krispies
1 c. chopped peanuts
1 c. semisweet chocolate chips
2 tbsp. shortening

Cream peanut butter and margarine in bowl. Add confectioners' sugar; blend well. Stir in cereal. Shape by level tablespoonfuls into logs; coat with peanuts. Melt chocolate and shortening in double boiler over hot water. Drizzle over logs. Chill until firm. Yield: 3¼ dozen.

Photograph for this recipe on page 6.

PEANUT BUTTER-FUDGE PINWHEELS

1 c. peanut butter chips
1 can sweetened condensed milk
1 c. semisweet chocolate chips
1 tsp. vanilla extract
½ c. chocolate sprinkles

Melt peanut butter chips in half the condensed milk in saucepan over low heat, stirring occasionally. Spread into 10x12-inch rectangle on cookie sheet lined with greased foil. Let stand for 30 minutes. Melt chocolate chips in remaining condensed milk in saucepan over low heat, stirring frequently; remove from heat. Stir in vanilla. Cool slightly. Spread over peanut butter layer. Let stand for 30 minutes. Roll as for jelly roll. Coat with sprinkles. Store, tightly wrapped, in refrigerator for up to 2 weeks. Bring to room temperature. Cut into ¼-inch slices. Yield: 4 dozen.

Ruth Fuller Lature, Kentucky

QUICK ENERGY PICKUPS

1 c. confectioners' sugar
1 c. crunchy peanut butter
1 c. semisweet chocolate chips
1 c. raisins
½ c. dry milk powder
⅔ c. coconut

Combine first 5 ingredients and 3 tablespoons water in bowl; mix well. Shape into balls. Roll in coconut. Yield: 7½ dozen.

Sue Knotts, West Virginia

EASY PECAN ROLL

1 12-oz. package penuche fudge mix
8 oz. caramels
¼ c. milk
1½ c. chopped pecans

Prepare fudge mix according to package directions. Shape into four 1-inch diameter rolls. Melt caramels with milk in saucepan over low heat, stirring constantly. Spread over rolls. Roll in pecans. Chill until firm. Cut into ½-inch slices. Yield: 1½ pounds.

Annette Campbell, Oklahoma

MASHED POTATO CANDY

¾ c. cold mashed potatoes
4 c. confectioners' sugar
4 c. shredded coconut
1½ tsp. vanilla extract

½ tsp. salt
8 sq. semisweet chocolate, melted

Mix potatoes and confectioners' sugar in bowl. Stir in coconut, vanilla and salt. Press into ½-inch layer in large dish. Spread melted chocolate over top. Cut into squares when cool. Yield: 3 pounds.

Nicky Peters, Georgia

EASY ROCKY ROAD SQUARES

2 8-oz. milk chocolate bars
3 c. miniature marshmallows
¾ c. coarsely chopped pecans

Melt chocolate in double boiler over hot water. Stir in marshmallows and pecans. Spread in buttered 8-inch square dish. Chill until firm. Cut into squares. Yield: 1½ pounds.

Photograph for this recipe on Cover.

MICROWAVE TOFFEE BARS

11 graham crackers
½ c. butter
½ c. packed brown sugar
½ c. confectioners' sugar
1 tbsp. cornstarch
¼ tsp. salt
1 c. flaked coconut
½ c. chopped pecans
1 6-oz. package semisweet chocolate chips

Arrange graham crackers to cover bottom of 8x12-inch glass baking dish. Combine butter and brown sugar in 1-quart casserole. Microwave on High for 2 minutes. Mix well. Add confectioners' sugar, cornstarch, salt, coconut and pecans; mix well. Spread evenly over graham crackers. Sprinkle with chocolate chips. Microwave on High for 2 to 2½ minutes. Let stand for several minutes. Spread melted chocolate evenly over top. Cut into squares. Cool.

Barbara Mitchell, Virginia

HOMEMADE TOOTSIE ROLLS

½ c. honey
1 tbsp. butter
¼ c. cocoa
1 to 1½ c. nonfat dry milk powder

Combine honey, butter and cocoa in bowl; mix well. Add enough dry milk powder to make firm dough. Knead until smooth. Shape into small rolls; place on waxed paper. Let stand until firm. Wrap each in waxed paper. Yield: 1 dozen.
Note: May omit cocoa and add 1 cup peanut butter to make candy which resembles Bit-O-Honey.

Doug Shaw, New Mexico

BUTTERCREAM TRUFFLES

4 sq. unsweetened chocolate
⅓ c. butter
2 c. sifted confectioners' sugar
4 egg yolks
1 tsp. vanilla extract
Ground toasted hazelnuts

Melt chocolate and butter in saucepan over very low heat, stirring constantly. Cool. Blend in confectioners' sugar. Add egg yolks 1 at a time, beating well after each addition. Add vanilla; mix well. Chill until firm. Drop by rounded teaspoonfuls into hazelnuts; roll to coat. Place in paper bonbon cups. Store, covered, in refrigerator. Yield: 1 pound.

Kathleen St.George, California

CHOCOLATE TRUFFLES

½ c. heavy cream
⅓ c. sugar
6 tbsp. butter
2 c. miniature semisweet chocolate chips
1 tsp. vanilla extract
1 tbsp. shortening
Finely chopped nuts
Shaved chocolate
Confectioners' sugar

Combine heavy cream, sugar and butter in saucepan. Bring to a boil; remove from heat. Add 1 cup chocolate chips immediately; stir until chips are melted. Add vanilla. Pour into bowl. Let stand until cool; stir occasionally. Chill, covered, for several hours. Melt 1 cup chocolate chips and shortening in saucepan. Shape chilled mixture into ½-inch balls. Roll in chopped nuts, shaved chocolate or confectioners' sugar or coat with melted chocolate. Yield: 3 dozen.

Barbara Grimes, Illinois

CHOCOLATE TRUFFLE SURPRISES

½ c. unsalted butter, softened
½ c. cocoa
2½ c. confectioners' sugar
¼ c. whipping cream
1½ tsp. vanilla extract
Mints, candied cherries, whole almonds,
    pecan or walnut halves (opt.)
Flaked coconut or chopped nuts (opt.)

Cream butter in bowl until light and fluffy. Add mixture of cocoa and confectioners' sugar alternately with cream and vanilla, blending well after each addition. Chill until firm. Shape into 1-inch balls around mints, cherries or nuts. Coat with coconut, chopped nuts or additional confectioners' sugar. Chill until firm. Yield: 3 dozen.

Photograph for this recipe on page 53.

ORANGE-CHOCOLATE TRUFFLES

2 Florida oranges, seeded, ground
8 oz. semisweet chocolate
¼ c. whipping cream
¼ c. butter
3 tbsp. sugar
1 12-oz. package vanilla wafers,
    finely crushed
Shredded coconut, confectioners' sugar
    or chopped nuts

Combine first 5 ingredients in saucepan. Cook over low heat for 10 minutes, stirring constantly. Remove from heat. Stir in crumbs. Chill until firm enough to handle. Shape into 1-inch balls. Roll in coconut, confectioners' sugar or nuts. Yield: 4 dozen.

Photograph for this recipe on page 87.

CHERRY-PEANUT BALLS

1 16-oz. package confectioners' sugar
1 package cherry frosting mix
¼ c. melted margarine
2 tsp. vanilla extract
½ can sweetened condensed milk
½ to 1 jar maraschino cherries, chopped
1 12-oz. package milk chocolate chips
2 to 3 tbsp. melted paraffin
8 oz. peanuts, ground (opt.)

Combine first 6 ingredients in bowl; mix well. Chill for several minutes. Shape into small balls; place on waxed paper. Freeze until firm. Melt chocolate chips in double boiler. Blend in paraffin. Stir in peanuts. Dip candy balls into chocolate; place in paper bonbon cups. Yield: 3 pounds.

Alice Keller, Iowa

◆◆◆◆◆◆◆◆◆◆◆◆◆◆◆◆◆◆◆◆◆◆◆◆◆◆

Hint: *To use melted chocolate chips for dipping, add a small amount of melted shortening or paraffin to speed set up. Paraffin sets up faster and is glossier while shortening yields a softer coating.*

◆◆◆◆◆◆◆◆◆◆◆◆◆◆◆◆◆◆◆◆◆◆◆◆◆◆

CHERRY-WALNUT BALLS

1 c. peanut butter
1 c. confectioners' sugar
1 c. chopped walnuts
1 c. chopped candied cherries
2 tbsp. butter, softened
1 8-oz. package semisweet chocolate
1 tbsp. melted paraffin

Combine peanut butter, confectioners' sugar, walnuts, cherries and butter in bowl; mix well. Shape into balls. Melt chocolate in double boiler. Blend in paraffin. Dip peanut butter balls into chocolate to coat. Place in paper bonbon cups. Yield: 2½ dozen.

Dona Miller, Canada

◆◆◆◆◆◆◆◆◆◆◆◆◆◆◆◆◆◆◆◆◆◆◆◆◆◆◆◆◆

Hint: *Dipping Temperatures for Chocolate:*
Real milk chocolate 86°
Real dark chocolate 90°
Chocolate coatings 98°

◆◆◆◆◆◆◆◆◆◆◆◆◆◆◆◆◆◆◆◆◆◆◆◆◆◆◆◆◆

CHOCOLATE-COVERED CHERRIES

1 lb. dark chocolate
2 to 3 tbsp. melted paraffin
1 16-oz. package confectioners' sugar
2 tbsp. evaporated milk
1 tsp. vanilla extract
1 lg. jar maraschino cherries with stems, drained

Melt chocolate in double boiler. Blend in paraffin. Mix confectioners' sugar, evaporated milk and vanilla in bowl. Shape by spoonfuls into balls around cherries. Dip into chocolate to coat. Place in paper bonbon cups. Yield: 5 dozen.

Marian Hart, Arizona

MOUND BONBONS

¾ c. unseasoned mashed potatoes
4 c. confectioners' sugar
4 c. shredded coconut
1 12-oz. package chocolate chips
2 to 3 tbsp. melted paraffin

Combine first 3 ingredients in bowl; mix well. Chill overnight. Shape into 1-inch balls. Melt chocolate chips in saucepan over low heat, stirring frequently. Blend in paraffin. Dip candy balls into chocolate. Place in paper bonbon cups. Yield: 2½ pounds.

Juanita Hall, Ohio

DIPPED CHERRY CANDY

1 2-lb. package confectioners' sugar
4 c. chopped pecans
1 c. chopped maraschino cherries
1 tsp. vanilla extract
1 sm. can flaked coconut
1 can sweetened condensed milk
½ c. melted margarine
1 12-oz. package chocolate chips
2 to 3 tbsp. melted paraffin

Combine first 7 ingredients in bowl; mix well. Chill until very firm. Shape into balls. Melt chocolate chips in double boiler. Blend in paraffin. Dip each ball in chocolate mixture; place in paper bonbon cups. Yield: 5½ pounds.

Peggy Haynes, Oklahoma

COCONUT-PECAN DROPS

2 16-oz. packages confectioners' sugar
2 c. chopped pecans
1 can sweetened condensed milk
1 can flaked coconut
1 tsp. vanilla extract
1 12-oz. package semisweet chocolate chips
2 to 3 tbsp. melted paraffin

Combine confectioners' sugar, pecans, condensed milk, coconut and vanilla in bowl; mix well. Shape into balls; place on waxed paper-lined plate. Chill until firm. Melt chocolate chips in double boiler over hot water. Blend in paraffin. Dip candy balls into chocolate to coat. Place in paper bonbon cups. Yield: 4½ pounds.

Jerri Williams, Georgia

COCONUT-ALMOND JOY BALLS

½ c. butter, softened
1 16-oz. package confectioners' sugar
1 3-oz. package cream cheese, softened
3 c. coconut
Whole almonds
1 12-oz. package chocolate chips

Cream butter and confectioners' sugar in bowl until light and fluffy. Add cream cheese and coconut; mix well. Shape into walnut-sized ball around each almond. Melt chocolate chips in double boiler. Dip half of each ball into chocolate. Place chocolate side up in paper bonbon cups. Yield: 6 dozen.

Bea Peterson, California

Recipes on pages 46, 85. ◆

BUTTER CREAMS

2 sticks butter, softened
1 8-oz. package cream cheese, softened
3 16-oz. packages confectioners' sugar
8-oz. semisweet chocolate
1 tbsp. melted butter
2 to 3 tbsp. melted paraffin
¼ tsp. vanilla extract

Cream butter and cream cheese in bowl until light and fluffy. Add confectioners' sugar gradually, beating until smooth after each addition. Chill in refrigerator. Shape into balls. Melt chocolate with butter in saucepan over low heat. Blend in paraffin and vanilla. Dip candy balls into chocolate to coat. Place in paper bonbon cups. Yield: 4½ pounds.

Nancy Sykes, Georgia

HAND-DIPPED CHOCOLATE CREAMS

3 16-oz. packages confectioners' sugar
2 3-oz. packages cream cheese, softened
6 tbsp. vanilla extract
1 c. plus 2 tbsp. butter, softened
3 6-oz. packages chocolate chips
1 4-oz. package German's chocolate
4 to 6 tbsp. melted paraffin

Cream confectioners' sugar, cream cheese, vanilla and butter in bowl until light and fluffy. Chill overnight. Shape into 1-inch balls. Place on waxed paper-lined tray. Chill overnight. Melt chocolate in double boiler over boiling water, stirring frequently. Blend in paraffin. Dip candy into chocolate; place in paper bonbon cups. Yield: 5 pounds.
Note: May substitute orange, mint or lemon extract or maple syrup for vanilla.

Allison Canfield, New York

MARTHA WASHINGTON CANDY

2 16-oz. packages confectioners' sugar, sifted
1 stick margarine, softened
1 can sweetened condensed milk
1 tsp. vanilla extract
4 c. chopped pecans
1 8-oz. package semisweet chocolate
2 to 3 tbsp. melted paraffin

Cream confectioners' sugar, margarine, condensed milk and vanilla in bowl until light and fluffy. Stir in pecans. Shape into walnut-sized balls. Melt chocolate in double boiler. Blend in paraffin. Dip candy balls into chocolate mixture. Place in paper bonbon cups. Yield: 4 pounds.

Claudia Cox, Alabama

◆ Recipes on pages 56, 90, 92.

CHOCOLATE-DIPPED MARSHMALLOWS

1 8-oz. milk chocolate bar
1 tsp. shortening
30 lg. marshmallows
Chopped peanuts (opt.)
Graham cracker crumbs (opt.)
Flaked coconut (opt.)

Melt chocolate and shortening in double boiler over hot water; blend well. Cool slightly. Dip marshmallows 1 at a time into chocolate using toothpicks. Coat with 1 of the optional ingredients. Place on waxed paper-lined plate. Chill for 15 minutes. Serve chilled. Yield: 2½ dozen.
Note: Add 1 to 2 teaspoons shortening if necessary to make chocolate of dipping consistency. Do not add milk, cream or water.

Photograph for this recipe on Cover.

MILLIONAIRES

1 14-oz. package caramels
2 tbsp. butter
3 c. whole pecans
1 6-oz. package chocolate chips
1 to 1½ tbsp. melted paraffin

Melt caramels and butter with 2 tablespoons water in saucepan over low heat, stirring frequently. Stir in pecans. Drop by spoonfuls onto waxed paper. Chill until firm. Melt chocolate chips in saucepan over low heat, stirring frequently. Blend in paraffin. Dip caramels into chocolate mixture; place in paper bonbon cups. Yield: 4 dozen.

JoAnn R. Sicking, Texas

PEANUT BUTTER PATTIES

1½ c. peanut butter
10 tbsp. honey
1 c. nonfat dry milk powder
Milk chocolate, melted

Combine peanut butter, honey and dry milk in bowl; mix well. Shape into long thin roll. Chill until firm. Cut into slices. Dip each slice in chocolate; place on waxed paper. Chill until firm. Yield: 1 pound.

Fern Heap, Utah

◆◆◆◆◆◆◆◆◆◆◆◆◆◆◆◆◆◆◆◆◆◆◆◆◆◆

Hint: For variety in coating chocolate, try different kinds and colors or tint white chocolate with food coloring

◆◆◆◆◆◆◆◆◆◆◆◆◆◆◆◆◆◆◆◆◆◆◆◆◆◆

KENTUCKY COLONELS

½ c. butter, softened
3 tbsp. sweetened condensed milk
⅓ c. Bourbon
7½ c. confectioners' sugar
½ c. chopped pecans
1   12-oz. package semisweet
    chocolate chips
2 tbsp. melted paraffin
Pecan halves

Combine first 4 ingredients in large bowl; mix well. Stir in chopped pecans. Shape into 1-inch balls. Melt chocolate chips with paraffin in double boiler, stirring frequently. Dip candy balls into chocolate; place in paper bonbon cups. Press pecan half into each. Yield: 3½ pounds.

Carol Stallard, Oklahoma

PEANUT BUTTER-MARSHMALLOW CREMES

1½ c. butter, softened
1   2-lb. package confectioners' sugar
1 c. peanut butter
1 c. marshmallow creme
1 tbsp. vanilla extract
1 lb. sweet chocolate
3 to 4 tbsp. melted paraffin

Cream butter and about 2 cups confectioners' sugar in bowl until light and fluffy. Add peanut butter, marshmallow creme and vanilla; blend well. Add remaining confectioners' sugar gradually, blending well. Shape into balls; place on waxed paper-lined tray. Chill overnight. Melt chocolate in double boiler. Blend in paraffin. Dip each candy cream in chocolate; place in paper bonbon cups. Yield: 4 pounds.

Jean Prince, Pennsylvania

REESE-TYPE BARS

1 c. peanut butter
½ c. melted butter
1¾ c. confectioners' sugar
3 tbsp. brown sugar
½ tsp. vanilla extract
¼ tsp. salt
1   6-oz. package chocolate chips
2 tbsp. oil

Combine first 6 ingredients with 2 tablespoons water in large bowl. Beat until well blended and mixture forms ball. Pat into 7x11-inch dish; smooth top. Melt

chocolate chips with oil in double boiler; mix well. Spread smoothly over peanut butter mixture. Let stand until set. Cut into squares. Yield: 2 pounds.

Audrey Smith, Illinois

CHOCOLATE STRAWBERRIES

1   6-oz. package semisweet chocolate
    chips
2 c. fresh strawberries

Melt chocolate in double boiler over hot water; remove from heat. Rinse strawberries; pat dry. Dip strawberries 1 at a time into chocolate, holding strawberries by stem ends. Place on waxed paper. Let stand until set.

Photograph for this recipe on page 78.

COCONUT FONDANT NESTS

1   16-oz. package confectioners' sugar,
    sifted
½ c. Karo light corn syrup
⅓ c. Mazola margarine
1 tsp. vanilla extract
2 drops of green food coloring
2   4-oz. packages shredded coconut
Miniature jelly beans

Combine 2 cups confectioners' sugar, corn syrup and margarine in 3-quart saucepan. Bring to a boil over medium-low heat, stirring constantly. Cool for 5 minutes. Stir in vanilla and food coloring. Beat with wooden spoon until slightly thickened. Stir in coconut just until moistened. Drop by heaping teaspoonfuls onto waxed paper-lined tray. Press jelly beans into center of each nest. Let stand until set. Store in tightly covered container. Yield: 2½ dozen.

Photograph for this recipe on page 88.

CRANBERRY-BUTTERSCOTCH FUDGE

2 c. sugar
¼ c. light corn syrup
1⅓ c. milk
⅓ c. light cream
1 tsp. vanilla extract
1 tbsp. butter
1¼ c. coarsely chopped pecans
1 c. Ocean Spray cranberries,
    coarsely chopped

Combine first 4 ingredients in large saucepan. Cook over medium heat until sugar dissolves, stirring constantly. Cook over medium-low heat to 238 degrees on candy thermometer, soft-ball stage, stirring down only if necessary. Remove from heat. Add vanilla and butter; do not stir. Cool to lukewarm, 110 degrees; do not stir. Beat until thickened and mixture loses its luster. Stir in pecans and cranberries. Pour into 8-inch square dish. Let stand until firm. Cut into 1-inch squares. Yield: 2½ pouds.

Photograph for this recipe on page 54.

CRANBERRY TURTLES

8 oz. creamy vanilla caramels
2 tbsp. cream
1¼ c. pecan halves
1 c. Ocean Spray cranberries
4 oz. semisweet chocolate, melted

Melt caramels with cream in double boiler over hot water. Cool for 10 minutes. Arrange pecan halves in clusters of 5 as for turtles on waxed paper-lined surface. Place 2 or 3 cranberries in center of each cluster. Pour 1 teaspoon caramel over each cluster. Let stand until firm. Spoon chocolate over caramel. Let stand until firm. Store between layers of waxed paper in airtight container. Yield: 2 dozen.

Photograph for this recipe on page 54.

DATE-MARSHMALLOW LOG

24 marshmallows, chopped
1½ c. chopped dates
3 c. chopped walnuts
45 graham crackers, crushed
1¼ c. heavy cream

Combine marshmallows, dates, walnuts and 2⅔ cups graham cracker crumbs in bowl; mix well. Add cream; mix well. Shape into log. Coat with remaining graham cracker crumbs. Wrap tightly in waxed paper. Chill until firm. Slice as desired. Yield: 2 pounds.

Charlotte Youree, Tennessee

NO-BAKE DATE BARS

1 lb. pitted dates, chopped
1½ c. shredded coconut
½ c. butter
¼ c. honey
2½ c. oats
⅔ c. chopped nuts
1 tsp. vanilla extract

Combine first 4 ingredients and ½ cup water in saucepan. Cook over medium heat until thick, stirring frequently. Add oats, nuts and vanilla; mix well.

Spread in buttered 9x13-inch pan. Chill for 2 hours. Cut into bars. Store in airtight container in refrigerator for several days.

Grace Hemingway, Missouri

FOREVER AMBERS

1 14-oz. package candy orange
    slices, chopped
1 can sweetened condensed milk
1 can flaked coconut
1 c. chopped pecans
1 tsp. orange extract
2 c. confectioners' sugar

Combine orange slices, condensed milk, coconut, pecans and orange extract in baking dish; mix well. Bake at 300 degrees until bubbly. Stir in confectioners' sugar. Drop by spoonfuls onto waxed paper. Let stand until firm. Yield: 2 dozen.

Dee Ann Williams, Texas

FOUR-FRUIT BALLS

8 oz. dried apricots
8 oz. prunes
2 slices candied pineapple
4 oz. candied cherries
1 c. nuts
1 c. honey
¾ c. confectioners' sugar

Put first 5 ingredients through finest blade of food grinder 2 times. Combine with honey in bowl; mix well. Shape into balls. Roll in confectioners' sugar. Store in airtight container in cool place. Yield: 1½ pounds.

Marilyn Gornto, Georgia

FRUITCAKE CANDY ROLL

1 c. chopped marshmallows
¾ c. chopped pecans
1 c. chopped dates
5 tbsp. sweetened condensed milk
¼ c. cherry juice
3 c. graham cracker crumbs

Combine first 3 ingredients in bowl; mix well. Add condensed milk and juice; mix well. Stir in crumbs. Shape into roll; wrap in plastic wrap. Chill for 12 hours or longer before slicing.

Pauline Kubina, Iowa

BROWN SUGAR KISSES

> 1 c. packed brown sugar, sifted
> 1 egg white, stiffly beaten
> 1 tsp. vanilla extract
> 1 c. pecan halves
> 1 tsp. salt

Add brown sugar to egg white gradually, beating constantly. Beat until very stiff peaks form. Stir in remaining ingredients. Drop by teaspoonfuls onto greased baking sheet. Place in preheated 375-degree oven. Turn oven off. Let stand in closed oven until cool. Yield: 1½ dozen.

Angie Rabroker, Texas

HOMEMADE MARSHMALLOWS

> 1 env. unflavored gelatin
> ½ c. sugar
> ⅔ c. light corn syrup
> 1 tsp. vanilla extract
> ⅓ tsp. salt
> Confectioners' sugar

Soften gelatin in ⅓ cup cold water in top of double boiler. Let stand for 5 minutes. Cook over boiling water until gelatin dissolves, stirring constantly. Add sugar, stirring until completely dissolved. Combine corn syrup, vanilla and salt in large mixer bowl. Add hot gelatin mixture. Beat at high speed for 15 minutes or until light and fluffy. Pour into lightly greased 9-inch square pan. Cool until set. Cut into squares. Roll each in confectioners' sugar. Yield: 3 dozen.

Bertha Probasco, Nevada

MARZIPAN EASTER EGGS

> 1 c. almond paste
> ¼ c. Karo light corn syrup
> ¼ c. Mazola margarine, softened
> ½ tsp. almond extract
> 1 16-oz. package confectioners' sugar
> 1 6-oz. package semisweet chocolate chips, melted
> 1 recipe Decorator's Frosting (see p. 52)

Combine first 4 ingredients in mixer bowl. Beat at medium speed until smooth. Add 1 cup confectioners' sugar; beat well. Stir in as much remaining confectioners' sugar as possible with wooden spoon. Knead in any remaining confectioners' sugar. Shape into 12 eggs; place on waxed paper-lined tray. Chill for several hours. Dip larger end of each egg into chocolate. Stand eggs chocolate end down on waxed paper-lined tray. Chill until firm. Decorate with Decorator's

Frosting as desired. Let stand until set. Store in airtight container in cool place. Yield: 1 dozen.

Photograph for this recipe on page 88.

PECAN-COVERED FRUIT BALLS

> 1 8-oz. package dried peaches, ground
> 1 c. pitted dates, ground
> 1 c. dark seedless raisins, ground
> 1 8-oz. package prunes, ground
> Pecans, finely chopped

Combine fruits in large bowl; mix well. Shape by teaspoonfuls into balls. Roll in pecans. Store in airtight container in refrigerator. Yield: 6 dozen.

Rosalind L. Woodard, Tennessee

CHEWY GRANOLA CRISPS

> 32 caramels
> ¼ c. margarine
> 1 tbsp. milk
> ¼ tsp. salt
> 2 c. granola
> 1 c. crisp rice cereal
> ½ c. raisins
> ½ to ¾ c. M and M's

Melt caramels and margarine with milk and salt in saucepan over low heat, stirring occasionally. Add gradually to mixture of cereals, raisins and candy in large greased bowl, tossing constantly until coated. Press into greased 9x13-inch pan. Let stand for 1 hour or until firm. Cut into bars.

Photograph for this recipe on this page.

FORGOTTEN MERINGUES

3 egg whites
1 c. sifted sugar
1 tsp. vanilla or peppermint extract
¾ c. chopped nuts (opt.)
¾ c. coconut (opt.)
¾ c. miniature chocolate chips (opt.)

Beat egg whites until soft peaks form. Add sugar gradually, beating until stiff peaks form. Fold in flavoring and nuts, coconut or chocolate chips. Drop by teaspoonfuls onto parchment-lined cookie sheet. Place in preheated 300-degree oven. Turn oven off. Let stand in closed oven for several hours. Peel off parchment. Store in covered container.
Yield: 6½ dozen.

Priscilla Teeter, Maryland

SWEDISH CRYSTAL NUTS

1½ c. whole blanched almonds
2 c. walnut halves
2 egg whites
1 c. sugar
Dash of salt
½ c. melted butter

Spread almonds and walnuts on baking sheet. Bake at 325 degrees until light brown. Beat egg whites until stiff peaks form. Fold in sugar and salt. Beat until very stiff. Fold in toasted nuts. Pour butter into 10x15-inch baking pan. Spread nut mixture in prepared pan. Bake at 325 degrees for 30 minutes, stirring every 10 minutes. Spread on paper towels to cool. Store in airtight container. Yield: 4 cups.

Ann Thorndike, Nebraska

CREAM MINTS

1 egg white, beaten
1 tbsp. cream
1 tsp. vanilla extract
3 drops of oil of peppermint
Food coloring (opt.)
1   16-oz. package confectioners' sugar.
1 tsp. (heaping) butter, softened

Combine first 5 ingredients in bowl; mix well. Add confectioners' sugar all at once; mix well. Add butter and enough additional confectioners' sugar to make of firm consistency. Shape into small balls. Place on waxed paper. Flatten slightly with fork dipped in confectioners' sugar. Let stand overnight. Store between layers of waxed paper in airtight container.
Yield: 12 dozen.

Sue Underwood, Virginia

HOMEMADE MINTS

4 oz. cream cheese, softened
½ tsp. oil of peppermint
Food coloring
3⅓ c. confectioners' sugar
Sugar

Blend cream cheese, oil of peppermint and food coloring in bowl. Add confectioners' sugar; knead until well mixed. Shape into marble-sized balls. Roll in sugar. Press into candy mold; remove immediately.
Yield: 7 dozen.

Diane Pretz, Washington

ALMOND BARK CONFECTIONS

1¾ c. almond bark
1 c. crunchy peanut butter
2 c. dry roasted peanuts
3 c. crisp rice cereal
2 c. miniature marshmallows

Melt almond bark and peanut butter in baking dish in 200-degree oven. Stir in peanuts, cereal and marshmallows. Drop by teaspoonfuls onto waxed paper. Cool. Store in cool place. Yield: 7½ dozen.

Rhonda Rydell, Texas

BREAKFAST BARS

½ c. butter
32 lg. marshmallows
½ c. peanut butter
½ c. nonfat dry milk powder
¼ c. orange-flavored instant breakfast
**   drink powder**
1 c. raisins
4 c. Cheerios

Melt butter and marshmallows in saucepan over low heat, stirring constantly. Stir in peanut butter. Cook until peanut butter melts, stirring constantly. Add dry milk and orange drink powder. Fold in raisins and cereal; mix until coated. Pat into buttered 9x13-inch dish. Let stand until firm. Cut into bars.
Yield: 2 dozen.

Lena Hollifield, North Carolina

CAMPING CANDY

1 c. packed brown sugar
1 c. light corn syrup
2 c. peanut butter
1 c. each oats, soy nuts, peanuts, raisins, granola and sunflower seed

Combine brown sugar and corn syrup in large saucepan. Boil for several minutes. Stir in peanut butter. Add remaining ingredients; mix well. Shape into small balls. Store in covered container. Yield: 4 pounds.
Note: May substitute mixture of ½ cup honey and ½ cup corn syrup for sweeteners.

Jeanette Laxton, Washington

DICTATION DROPS

½ c. margarine
2 c. sugar
½ c. milk
¾ c. peanut butter
3 c. quick-cooking oats

Melt margarine in large saucepan over medium heat. Add sugar and milk. Bring to a boil. Cook for 2 minutes, stirring constantly. Remove from heat. Stir in peanut butter. Add oats; mix well. Drop by teaspoonfuls onto waxed paper-lined tray. Chill until set. Yield: 4 dozen.

Betty C. Nutt, Tennessee

SIX-CUP MAGIC

1 c. peanut butter
1 c. nonfat dry milk powder
1 c. sugar
1 c. light corn syrup
1 c. raisins, coconut or chocolate chips
1 c. (or more) graham cracker crumbs

Combine all ingredients except graham cracker crumbs in large bowl; mix well. Shape into small balls. Roll in graham cracker crumbs. Yield: 3 dozen.

Emily Owen, Tennessee

PEANUT BUTTER BALLS

½ c. peanut butter
¼ c. honey
½ c. (or more) nonfat dry milk powder
1 tbsp. sunflower seed
1 tbsp. chopped walnuts
1 tbsp. chopped raisins
3 tbsp. sesame seed

Combine peanut butter and honey in bowl; mix well. Add milk powder gradually, mixing until of bread dough consistency. Stir in next 3 ingredients. Shape into small balls. Roll in sesame seed. Chill in refrigerator. Yield: 1½ dozen.

Marie Delffs, Tennessee

PEANUT BUTTER WHIRLS

1 med. potato, cooked, mashed
2½ to 3½ c. confectioners' sugar
Chunky peanut butter

Combine warm potato with enough confectioners' sugar to make medium dough. Roll ¼ inch thick. Spread with peanut butter. Roll as for jelly roll. Chill in refrigerator. Cut into slices. Yield: 1 pound.

Ruby Boyd, Colorado

PUTTERFINGERS

½ c. melted margarine
3 c. oats
1 c. honey
3 tbsp. carob powder
¾ c. nonfat dry milk powder
½ tsp. salt
2 tsp. vanilla extract
½ c. peanut butter
½ c. raisins
½ c. sunflower seed (opt.)

Combine margarine and oats in large bowl; mix well. Add remaining ingredients; mix well. Shape as desired. Chill until firm. Wrap in waxed paper and foil. Yield: 2 pounds.
Note: Putterfingers are easily made by children who like to "putter" in the kitchen and make nutritious snacks or nice gifts. They are good for school lunches or outings.

Pat Miller, Oregon

GEORGIA PECAN LOG

1 6-oz. package butterscotch chips, melted
⅓ c. sweetened condensed milk
½ tsp. vanilla extract
⅓ c. chopped pecans
1 egg white, lightly beaten
Pecan halves

Combine first 4 ingredients in bowl; mix well. Chill until firm enough to handle. Shape into 12-inch log on waxed paper. Score surface lengthwise with fork;

brush with egg white. Press pecan halves into roll to cover. Chill, wrapped in waxed paper, until firm. Cut into ½-inch slices. Yield: ¾ pound.

Jeanette Deupree, Georgia

PECAN LOGS

1   16-oz. package confectioners' sugar
1   7-oz. jar marshmallow creme
2   tsp. vanilla extract
1   14-oz. package caramels
⅓ c. evaporated milk
3 c. chopped pecans

Combine confectioners' sugar, marshmallow creme and vanilla in bowl; mix well. Shape into 4 logs on waxed paper-lined plate. Melt caramels with evaporated milk in double boiler over hot water, stirring occasionally. Spoon caramel over logs to coat. Coat with pecans. Cut into slices. Yield: 3½ pounds.

Jane Walker, Texas

KARMEL KORN

2 c. packed light brown sugar
½ c. light corn syrup
2 sticks butter
⅛ tsp. cream of tartar
1½ tsp. soda
6 qt. popped popcorn

Combine brown sugar, corn syrup, butter and cream of tartar in saucepan. Bring to a boil. Cook for 5 minutes. Add soda; mix well. Pour over popcorn in shallow baking pan. Bake at 200 degrees for 1 hour, stirring occasionally. Remove from oven. Cool. Store in airtight container. Yield: 24 cups.
Note: May press warm popcorn mixture into pan, cool and cut into squares; or shape into balls.

Jane McEllhiney Stein, California

SNOWCAPPED STRAWBERRIES

1 egg white
¾ c. sugar
1½ tsp. light corn syrup
⅛ tsp. salt
½ tsp. vanilla extract
4 c. fresh strawberries

Combine first 4 ingredients and ¼ cup water in double boiler; beat well. Place over rapidly boiling water. Beat at high speed with electric mixer until stiff peaks form. Remove from heat. Add vanilla. Beat until of spreading consistency. Rinse strawberries; pat dry.

Dip strawberries 1 at a time into mixture, holding strawberries by stem ends. Place on waxed paper. Let stand until set.

Photograph for this recipe on page 78.

PEANUTTY POPCORN SQUARES

½ c. sugar
½ c. light corn syrup
½ c. peanut butter
½ tsp. vanilla extract
3 c. popped popcorn
1 c. salted Spanish peanuts

Combine sugar and corn syrup in saucepan. Bring to a full boil; remove from heat. Stir in peanut butter and vanilla until smooth. Pour over mixture of popcorn and peanuts; stir to coat. Pat firmly into buttered 8-inch square pan. Cool. Cut into squares.

Hazel Davis, Wisconsin

QUICK CARAMEL CORN

2 tbsp. light corn syrup
¼ c. melted margarine
¼ c. packed brown sugar
3 qt. popped popcorn

Combine corn syrup and margarine in saucepan. Stir in brown sugar. Bring to a boil. Pour over popcorn; mix well. Cool. Yield: 12 cups.

Beth A. Archer, Ohio

RUM BALLS

2 sticks butter
1   16-oz. package confectioners' sugar
½ to 1 c. rum
1 angel food cake, trimmed,
    cut into 1-in. cubes
2 c. fine vanilla wafer crumbs
2 c. finely ground pecans

Combine butter, sugar and rum in double boiler. Cook until well blended, stirring constantly. Dip cake cubes in mixture; roll in mixture of crumbs and pecans. Place in paper bonbon cups. Store in airtight container in cool place. Let ripen before serving. Yield: 8 dozen.

Evelyn Brown, Tennessee

◆◆◆◆◆◆◆◆◆◆◆◆◆◆◆◆◆◆◆◆◆◆◆◆◆◆◆◆◆◆

Hint: *Dipping chocolate or chocolate coatings may be purchased in supermarkets and specialty shops. Chocolate of these types has been tempered by the manufacturer and will require melting according to package directions.*

◆◆◆◆◆◆◆◆◆◆◆◆◆◆◆◆◆◆◆◆◆◆◆◆◆◆◆◆◆◆

Glossary
Cookie & Candy Terms

Almond paste — mixture of finely ground blanched almonds and sugar which is used as ingredient in cookies and candies.

Amorphous or noncrystalline candy — chewy or hard candy that solidifies when cool, such as caramels, taffies and brittles.

Baking powder — leavening agent used in cookies, cakes and quick breads.

Baking soda — leavening agent used in cookies, cakes and quick breads. Soda is frequently used in combination with baking powder for crisp cookies.

Brittle — hard candy containing nuts which is poured into thin layer and cracked into pieces when cool.

Butter — butter is available in salted and unsalted forms. Unsalted or sweet butter is preferred for candy making.

Butterscotch — butter-flavored caramel candy which is sometimes cooked a little longer and dropped by spoonfuls onto waxed paper.

Candy tests — stages to which candy is cooked corresponding to candy thermometer temperature ranges.

> *Thread stage* — first stage in candy making in which sugar syrup reaches temperature of 230 to 234 degrees and forms at least 2-inch thread when dropped from spoon.
>
> *Soft-ball stage* — syrup reaches temperature of 234 to 240 degrees and a small amount dropped into very cold water forms a soft ball that flattens when removed from water. Fondants and fudges are cooked to this stage.
>
> *Firm-ball stage* — syrup reaches 240 to 248 degrees and a small amount dropped into very cold water forms a firm ball that holds shape when removed from water. Caramels are cooked to this stage.
>
> *Hard-ball stage* — syrup reaches 250 to 268 degrees and a small amount dropped into very cold water forms hard ball that retains shape and is still pliable. Divinities, marshmallows and some taffies are cooked to this stage.
>
> *Soft-crack stage* — syrup reaches 270 to 290 degrees and a small amount dropped into very cold water separates into hard but not brittle threads. Taffies and butterscotch are cooked to this stage.
>
> *Hard-crack stage* — syrup reaches 300 to 310 degrees and a small amount dropped into very cold water separates into hard brittle threads. Brittles are cooked to this stage.

Candy thermometer — thermometer made especially for candy making. Thermometer should be calibrated before each use by placing in boiling water and noting variation from 212 degrees (boiling point of water).

Caramel — candy of chewy consistency made with butter and cream, poured into buttered pan, and cut into pieces when set.

Caramelized sugar — sugar heated over low heat until melted and golden brown.

Chocolate — product of the cocoa bean in many forms.

> *Baking* — unsweetened chocolate packaged in 1-ounce squares or 1-ounce envelopes in premelted form.

> *Cocoa* — powdered form of unsweetened chocolate from which cocoa butter has been removed.

> *Dipping* — pretempered chocolate which requires only melting.

> *German's* — sweet cooking chocolate packaged in 4-ounce bars. Named for Mr. German who began mixing chocolate with sugar before packaging.
> *Milk* — mixture of processed cocoa powder and cocoa butter.

> *Semisweet* — mixture of 60% unsweetened chocolate and 40% sugar which is packaged in 1-ounce squares or as chocolate chips.

> *Tempered* — milk chocolate prepared for candy dipping by melting, cooling and heating to dipping temperature.

Cookies — tasty treats for all occasions.

> *Bar* — batter is poured or pressed into rectangular pan, baked, cooled and cut into bars or squares.

> *Drop* — batter is dropped by spoonfuls onto cookie sheet. Drops should be of uniform size for uniform baking with enough space between for spreading. Drops may be flattened with fork, glass or heel of hand.

> *Pressed* — dough is pressed through cookie press fitted with any of several plates of varying design onto ungreased cookie sheet. Cookies may be tinted and/or decorated with tiny candies, colored sugar or fruit.

> *Refrigerator* — dough is usually shaped into loaf or roll then refrigerated or frozen until firm enough to slice.

> *Rolled* — dough is rolled on lightly floured surface with rolling pin and cut into shapes with knife or cookie cutter. Cookies should be cut close together to avoid the rerolling which results in less tender cookies.

> *Shaped* — firm dough is molded by hand into balls, crescents, twists, etc.

Cookie sheet — rimless or shallow-sided baking pan especially for non-bar cookies made of smooth shiny metal with or without nonstick coating. Size should be at least 2 inches smaller in each direction than oven rack for best heat circulation.

Corn syrup — sweetener used in making candy, glazes, etc. Both light and dark corn syrup may be used interchangeably depending on color and flavor desired.

Creaming — process of blending softened shortening and sugar in bowl with wooden spoon or electric mixer until light and fluffy in texture and appearance.

Crystalline candy — smooth creamy candy in which sugar crystals are too small to be seen or felt. Crystalline candies include fondant, fudge and divinity.

Cutting in — process of mixing flour and other dry ingredients and shortening using pastry blender or table knives to produce crumbly mixture.

Divinity — fluffy candy made by beating hot cooked sugar syrup into stiffly beaten egg whites then dropped by spoonfuls onto waxed paper.

Flour — unless otherwise specified, use all-purpose flour. Unbleached flour is interchangeable. Many recipes use whole wheat or other less refined flours but measurements are not interchangeable with all-purpose.

Fondant — confection base for mints, bonbons and creamy centers for chocolates. Fondant should be smooth and creamy. A ripening period after mixing improves handling and flavor.

Food coloring — primary colors that may be mixed as desired. Liquid colors are most common, but paste colors should be used for candy making when liquid measurements are critical.

Fudge — creamy smooth candy or confection of many varieties—chocolate, peanut butter, etc.

Honey — liquid sweetener extracted from honeycombs. Use oiled utensils for more precise measuring.

Macaroon — cookie made of finely chopped or ground nuts or coconut bound together with sweetened stiffly beaten egg whites.

Maple sugar — made from evaporation of sap of sugar maple trees. Usually pressed into fancy shapes for serving as confection.

Maple syrup — liquid sweetener resulting from evaporation of sap of sugar maple trees. Maple-flavored syrup is a blend of maple syrup and corn or sugar syrups.

Meringue — cookie made of mixture of egg whites and sugar which is very stiffly beaten until sugar is completely dissolved. Nuts, coconut, chocolate chips, etc. may be folded in gently. Mixture is dropped by spoonfuls onto cookie sheet lined with baking parchment then baked until firm and lightly browned. Sometimes called kiss.

Milk — many forms for various uses.

> *Buttermilk* — liquid from which butter fat has been removed by churning or which is commercially produced by adding cultures. Used interchangeably with sour milk.

> *Evaporated milk* — canned whole milk from which over half the water has been removed.

> *Nonfat dry milk powder* — powder remaining when water and butterfat have been removed from milk. Addition of water according to package directions yields skim milk for cooking or drinking. Dry powder is frequently added to recipes to increase nutritional values.

> *Sweetened condensed milk* — canned whole milk from which water has been removed and to which sugar has been added.

> *Whole milk* — fresh milk containing about 4% butterfat. Fresh milk of lesser butterfat content is called *skim milk*.

Mocha — mixture of chocolate and coffee flavors.

Molasses — thick liquid sweetener of varying color and flavor resulting from process of refining cane, beet or sorghum extracts into sugar.

Nougat — chewy candy made by adding a cooked syrup to stiffly beaten egg whites, then adding chopped almonds and pouring into dish. Let stand for several hours then cut into squares or rectangles.

Penuche — candy made in manner of fudge using brown sugar, poured into dish, and cut into squares when set.

Praline — nut candy similar to penuche which is dropped by spoonfuls into 3 to 4-inch patties.

Seafoam — candy made in same manner as divinity but using brown sugar.

Sugar — Commonly white granulated form for cooking and table use. Prepared by refining raw sugar to remove molasses.

> *Brown sugar* — less refined than white sugar, varies with the amount of molasses retained. Brown sugar was not packed for measuring in very old recipes but must always be firmly packed in modern recipes.

> *Confectioners' sugar* — fine powdery sugar made from grinding and sifting granulated sugar. Frequently a small amount of cornstarch is added to prevent caking. Also called powdered sugar or 10X sugar. Used mostly for frostings and coatings.

Taffy — candy cooked to hard-ball or soft-crack stage, cooled, pulled by hand until creamy and firm, then cut into pieces.

Wire rack — metal grid of thin wires and spaces permitting circulation of air on all sides for cooling cakes, cookies, etc., in or out of baking pans.

Index

All microwave recipe page numbers are preceded by an M.

Cookies

COOKBOOK ORDER FORM
Favorite Recipes Press

BOOK TITLE	Item#	Qty.	Price	Total
Postage & Handling	99929		$1.95	$1.95
Subtotal				
Add state & local tax				
Total Payment				

cc

**To place your charge card orders,
call our toll-free number
1-800-251-1542
or clip and mail convenient order form.**

Name _____

Address _____

City _____ State _____ Zip _____

Daytime Phone (___) _____

☐ Payment enclosed.

☐ Please Charge My: ☐ MasterCard   ☐ Visa

Expiration Date _____

Account Number _____

Signature _____

♦ No COD orders please.
♦ Prices subject to change without notice.
♦ Books offered subject to availability.
♦ Make checks payable to Great American Opportunities.

**Please mail completed
order form to:**

**Great American Opportunities, Inc.
P. O. Box 77, Nashville, TN 37202**